THE BIG PAYBACK

by the same editors

Access All Areas: The Diversity Manifesto
for TV and Beyond

Black British Lives Matter:
A Clarion Call for Equality

THE BIG PAYBACK

THE CASE FOR REPARATIONS FOR SLAVERY AND HOW THEY WOULD WORK

LENNY HENRY & MARCUS RYDER

faber

First published in 2025
by Faber & Faber Limited,
The Bindery, 51 Hatton Garden,
London EC1N 8HN

Typeset by Samantha Matthews
Printed and bound by CPI Group (UK) Ltd, Croydon, CR0 4YY

All rights reserved
© Lenny Henry and Marcus Ryder, 2025

The right of Lenny Henry and Marcus Ryder to be identified
as authors of this work has been asserted in accordance with Section 77
of the Copyright, Designs and Patents Act 1988

A CIP record for this book
is available from the British Library

ISBN 978–0–571–38001–5

Printed and bound in the UK on FSC® certified paper in line with our continuing
commitment to ethical business practices, sustainability and the environment.
For further information see faber.co.uk/environmental-policy

Our authorised representative in the EU for product safety is
Easy Access System Europe, Mustamäe tee 50, 10621 Tallinn, Estonia
gpsr.requests@easproject.com

2 4 6 8 10 9 7 5 3 1

This is for my colleagues at the Sir Lenny Henry Centre for Media Diversity at Birmingham City University. They are smart, kind and incredibly supportive of this work. Thanks to all.
Sir Lenny Henry

This book is dedicated to my son, Moses. May he, and all Black children, come to adulthood in a world freer and less racist than the one we live in today.
Marcus Ryder

CONTENTS

Introduction   1

  1: Flags, Chains and Truth   7
  2: British Slavery Ended 1 February 2015   15
  3: Humpty Dumpty's Problem with Definitions   27
  4: The End of Racism   39
  5: What Did Slavery Ever Do for Us?   49
  6: Doing the Maths   62
  6.5: Sins of Our Fathers (and Mothers)   73
  7: Reparations Versus Charity   84
  8: Making Wakanda a Reality   94
  9: Don't Mention the War   107
  10: The Trillion-dollar Question (Plus Another 20-ish Trillion)   121
  10.5: Not Every Dumpling Makes the Soup   134
  11: The Name's Lenny, Spelt with a Silent 'K'   140
  12: What Next?   150

  What Can We Do?   158

The Big Payback: The Play   161
A Note from Lenny   163
The Script   165
Acknowledgements   203
Further Reading   205
Notes   207

INTRODUCTION

Recently, I've read a lot about the idea of reparations being paid to Black people today for the crimes committed against our ancestors who survived transatlantic slavery.

I first became aware of the idea in the 1980s after film director Spike Lee named his production company '40 Acres and a Mule'. That was the compensation that in 1865 was promised to the families of freed slaves in America. Needless to say, the order was overturned, and they received nothing. On discovering this failed governmental promise, I began to think about whether we actually did deserve some sort of compensation.

Fast-forward three decades to 2014 when prominent African American author and journalist, Ta-Nehisi Coates, wrote an essay in *The Atlantic* titled 'The Case for Reparations'. Coates primarily focused on the experience of African Americans but his words had a seismic ripple effect worldwide.

Although the idea of reparations has been around for centuries – even before the end of the transatlantic slave trade – it was, perhaps, this one essay that catapulted it into the public discourse in the last ten years.

And then George Floyd was murdered. It seemed as though the entire world watched his death repeatedly on their laptops, mobile phones and news repeats.

Black Lives Matter protests swept the globe; my friends, family and colleagues debated the idea of reparations – surely this was the moment for change? The murmur that Coates's idea had brought into the public discourse became a roar.

While I've been writing mainly for theatre and television over the past few years, the argument for reparations has been constantly on my mind. These two things may, at first, seem totally unrelated, but as a therapist might put it: 'We can discover connections in the most unexpected places and that is normally when the breakthroughs happen.' I don't know which genius came up with this stuff personally, but I'd hate to meet them at a jumble sale.

One of the ways I have always processed how I feel about difficult subject matter has been through writing about them, either in the form of jokes or, more recently, as a screenwriter. I have worked in show business since I was a teenager and thankfully my writing has continually helped me unscramble challenging thoughts and ideas and concepts. Creativity has always been my 'safe space'.

So when we decided to finally look at the issue of reparations, I knew that my contribution should be to write a play or performance piece.

Writing a play about a subject I care about enables me to see things from other people's perspectives; I have to inhabit the characters as best I can as I write. The ability to create a coherent story with a beginning, middle and end is also important. If I can create something that makes sense it usually means I've understood the issue, at least to the extent I can talk about it publicly. A play can also humanise a debate; a 'town hall' meeting where disgruntled punters yell at their leaders is one way to unpick a knotty problem, but I'd rather watch a play and learn that way. Also, a play has to end. It gives me closure. I did not want to begin looking at these difficult issues without knowing that I would get closure at some point.

INTRODUCTION

The last play I wrote, *August in England*, was about the Windrush Scandal – the illegal deportation of people who legally came to the UK from the Caribbean in the 1950s and 1960s, named the 'Windrush generation' after the ship that brought the first wave of migrants from the West Indies after the Second World War.

I also wrote a TV series called *Three Little Birds*, about the racism and struggles Black people faced when they first settled in the UK.

Both shows were a form of catharsis for me. They not only gave me a deeper understanding of my family's history but also a perspective from which I could judge these complicated issues.

The truth is, until I can put something in a narrative, I cannot fully understand it.

I also realised that for such a big task I needed help. So I called up my friend and writing colleague Marcus Ryder. The American founding father Benjamin Franklin is supposed to have said, 'If you want something done, ask a busy person.' Well, Marcus fits that description perfectly and we've been working together on speeches and books on race and racism for over ten years. (Benjamin Franklin owned slaves, but also published pamphlets calling for an end to slavery – I told you this story is complex.)

Marcus once told me, 'We argue in anecdotes, we believe in narrative,' which roughly translates as: 'When we argue, we pick and choose examples that suit our argument, but to fully understand something we need to fit it into our belief structure about how the world works.' That's deeper than deep.

I embarked on the process of writing a play about reparations.

And when I told my publishers I was writing a play they asked if I could collect my notes into a book, documenting my journey into understanding the issues. I've given it my best shot and you'll find the playtext at the back of this book. It's called

The Big Payback and is a work in progress. I'd love to see it performed one day – but you never know.

I'd like to thank Marcus for his patience whilst I took big gaps in the writing process for this book because I had to figure out the play at the same time.

So while we're talking about plays, let me break down the classic way of thinking about a script.

Every character in a play or script has to be there for a reason. That reason is their narrative function: Aaron Sorkin talks about characters and their intention and obstacle. Who they are and what they desire and then the subtext of what they actually need is tied to the plot. The characters must state their intention and then use strategies to face and overcome the obstacles that stand in their way. Joseph Campbell called this process 'the Hero's Journey'. So in trying to understand the concept of reparations, I've chosen to work out the questions I need answering – the challenges and obstacles – and then invent a central character and surrounding cast that will enable me to explore them. Simples.

To start with, the questions I needed to answer were simple enough:

- What exactly are reparations?
- I've been fighting racism all my life – are reparations part of this fight or a distraction?
- How much are Black people owed?
- Are reparations only for Black people who are descendants of the transatlantic slave trade?
- Should Black people from Africa who experienced the horrors of colonialism, and not slavery, be entitled to reparations? And what about descendants of people who suffered other historical injustices?

INTRODUCTION

- Who should pay reparations? Should it be individuals? Corporations? Or governments?
- Can I answer the eternal philosophical question of whether any group is responsible for the sins of their fathers (and mothers) and is another group deserving of compensation for crimes committed against their forefathers and foremothers over a century ago?
- And finally, how would it all work? Would I get a cheque in the post or would I become owner of a National Trust house that was built with the proceeds of the profits of sugar plantations?

And there I had it.

I had my questions that needed answering and I was on a mission to understand one of the biggest ideas facing Black people in the world today.

I checked that my good friend Marcus Ryder was available – and you are now holding the results of our journey. Check out the playtext at the back of the book and see how my lead character, a white TV star, reacts when he discovers that his ancestors were involved in the slave trade and owned plantations. His discovery sets him on a journey that takes him from Los Angeles to Acocks Green in Birmingham, where he meets descendants of his forefathers' captive workforce.

Our objective was to get to grips with an idea that we both morally agree with – that wronged people should receive compensation – but which we have serious questions about on a practical level.

One last thing – Marcus and I both write to music. When I started to write I stuck a playlist on random and James Brown's 'The Payback' blasted out of my speakers. This was fate – I now had the title of the book *and* the play.

Hang on, Marcus wants to say something directly to you. Here he is:

Marcus: Throughout the book we refer to the 'transatlantic slave trade', the transportation of enslaved Africans to the Americas by Europeans for profit, between the sixteenth and nineteenth centuries. We use the term to refer not just to the trade itself but also to the whole practice of 'chattel slavery' of African people by Europeans. Chattel slavery is a system where one person has complete ownership of another, and enslaved people can be bought, sold, inherited, and their children are the property of the enslaver.

Lenny: Thanks, Marcus. I get it now. So are you ready? Then let's go for it.

1: FLAGS, CHAINS AND TRUTH

The year 2012 was interesting for all of us – particularly if we were part of the Windrush generation. Theresa May was Home Secretary at the time and had been quoted as saying she wanted to 'create, here in Britain, a really hostile environment for illegal immigration' – the beginning of the Windrush Scandal which inspired me to write my first ever play, *August in England*, for the Bush Theatre. I was also making *Rudy's Rare Records* for BBC Radio and going to Africa to make an appeal film for Comic Relief and Red Nose Day. Busy times – but not so busy that I couldn't pop back to my home town and open the local history centre. It was here that the actions of a small eleven-year-old white girl would turn my world upside down and start me on a path that would lead to me rethinking my place in the world, my place in history and what 'home' means to me.

Ultimately, this event triggered this book you're reading today (or maybe you're just in Waterstones flipping through it before buying something else. Hey you, don't buy that – buy this!!). It made me consider the idea that all Black British people, including all the descendants of the victims of the transatlantic slave trade, need reparations for slavery. I'll bet that's got your motor running.

OK, first . . . a little context.

I was born on 29 August 1958 in a market town about nine miles outside Birmingham called Dudley. If you're unfamiliar with British geography, Dudley is in the West Midlands, in the part locals refer to as the 'Black Country'. Now before anybody gets too excited, shocked or offended, the term 'Black Country' has nothing to do with race. Although I'm pretty sure my parents moved to this region for this very reason. 'But stop! The English people make a place just for Black people. Pack the dominoes, we're leaving right away!'

In the nineteenth century, that part of the world was Britain's industrial heartland; people referred to the area as the 'Black Country' in reference to the smoke and smog that originated from the thousands of foundries and forges that were spread across the region, along with the working of shallow coal seams.

For over a century, the area had no clear boundaries and it is said that 'no two Black Country men or women will agree on where it starts or ends'.[1]

After some research (Latin for 'Marcus found out this stuff'), I discovered that this informality around borders seemed to change around the turn of the century with the founding of the Black Country Consortium in 1999, and twelve years later with the founding of the Black Country Local Enterprise Partnership in 2011. These officially defined the Black Country as the four metropolitan boroughs of Dudley, Sandwell, Walsall and Wolverhampton, with an approximate area of 138 square miles.

Then, on 16 February 2012, an historical and cultural collection of artefacts from the area, held by the Black Country Living Museum (established in 1978), was awarded 'Designated' status by Arts Council England, recognising its quality and national significance.

I write all this to give you a little context of what was happening when that eleven-year-old-girl inadvertently transformed the way I see the world and set me off on my long journey to understand how I feel about reparations for slavery.

By 2012 the importance of the Black Country's place in British history was being officially recognised, causing much pride for the locals and myself, obviously. Come on, Dudley!

So, it was against this background that the Black Country Living Museum held a competition to design an official flag for the Black Country. This was part of a larger campaign by the Parliamentary Flags and Heraldry Committee to 'promote the flying of the Union Flag and flags associated with the UK, British territories, dependencies, Commonwealth, heraldry, British symbols and related issues'[2] – to encourage communities and regions to develop their own flags to celebrate the Diamond Jubilee of Elizabeth II and the 2012 Summer Olympics.

The response to the competition was massive: never underestimate the civic pride that Midlanders have in the Black Country. NEVER!

The best entrants were put up for a public vote with over 1,500 votes being cast by members of the public. A young local girl was announced as the winner at the Black Country Living Museum's Festival of Steam, celebrating 300 years of the Newcomen atmospheric engine.

The flag's design is simple and yet powerful; it is really clever and I can definitely understand why it won. It is in three sections of black, white and red. The red and black colours represent the famous furnaces of the region's industrial past and the infamous smoke that accompanied it.

The white section in the middle at first looks like a simple triangle but when you look closer it is actually cone-shaped, which is the architectural design of the iron furnaces that dotted the landscape of the area.

Finally, there is an interlinked chain that runs across the flag. The chain celebrates the manufacturing past of the region.

The Black Country was famous for making anchor and marine chains, which were used throughout the British Empire's rise to global prominence. The area was also famously responsible for making the chains and anchor for the *Titanic*.

The flag was officially unveiled in 2012 and the small schoolgirl, Gracie Sheppard, was rightly proud of being proclaimed the winner. Everybody celebrated.

This, ostensibly, is a typical story of local pride, a celebration of local history and, on the face of it, quite innocuous.

Let's cut to two years later where I enter the story: because I'm relatively famous in the Black Country, every so often I get asked to cut ribbons, appear at soirées and make speeches and whatnot. Often people of a certain age just want me to say the word OOOOKAAAAY for as long as I can. (If you know about *Tiswas*, you know . . .)

Long story short: on 23 April 2014 – two years after the Black Country flag officially came into existence – I found myself doing the 'local celebrity thing' by opening the Dudley Archives and Local History Centre on Tipton Road.

It's not quite the Oscars red carpet, but the local press were there and they wanted to take pictures of me by the swanky entrance. As I posed for the local photographers, I was handed the Black Country flag to hold. Until then, I hadn't really thought about the flag or its design.

Now, I don't know why this happened; maybe it was because I was thinking about the area's history and my place in it that something just clicked. I looked down at the flag I was holding and it slowly dawned on me that the chain on the flag didn't just represent those chains built for ships such as the *Titanic*. It also represented the shackles made to hold my enslaved ancestors on slave ships.

During this ceremony, whilst noticing the whole chain connection, I had an actual out-of-body experience.

If you Google 'Lenny Henry Black Country flag', you will find a picture of me smiling in front of the Dudley Archives and History Centre, arms outstretched, holding the flag in front of me.

Although I looked happy-go-lucky and smiley, inside I was thinking, 'What am I doing? I'm waving a flag celebrating the Black Country's history of making chains – some of which were utilised in the enslaving my ancestors!?'

And then my mind really began spinning off: 'I am so proud to be born in Dudley and to claim my identity of coming from the Black Country. But is the Black Country proud of me? Does this flag accept my place in the region's rich history?'

A therapist would describe what I was going through as disassociation – the mental process of disconnecting from one's thoughts, feelings, memories or sense of identity, as a way of coping with stress and trauma. My body was doing one thing – posing, smiling, cracking gags – meanwhile, a vast number of thoughts and feelings were racing through my mind. And could there be a more accurate description of how Black people feel about slavery than 'coping with stress and trauma'?

It is strange, but at no point did I think of refusing to hold the flag or telling the organisers why I was uncomfortable about the chains on the flag. I definitely didn't let on that I was having a mini breakdown about slavery and my African enslaved ancestors.

In my heart of hearts, I just think I didn't want to make a fuss. (How British of me.) I didn't want to remind people that a part of the country's history that *they* wanted to celebrate was deeply troubling for *me*. I didn't want them to feel uncomfortable about my trauma. And, probably most of all, I didn't want to seem like 'that kind of Black guy' who goes on about slavery and racism. The guy that people listen to sympathetically, but don't actually want to talk to.

It was as if I was more embarrassed about the region's connections to slavery than anyone else there and I would just be ruining this joyous moment if I mentioned it.

After the photos were taken I simply handed back the flag and didn't say a word to anyone. Most importantly, I didn't even talk to myself about it. I just bottled it all up. I did what I suspect is possibly the most mentally unhealthy thing anyone can do. This is one of the most common responses Black people have to our shared history and trauma of slavery.

In normal circumstances, that would have been the end of the story.

But a year later a fellow Black person from the Black Country picked up the mantle.

Patrick Vernon OBE was born in Wolverhampton, less than ten miles from Dudley. He is three years younger, but similar to me in that his parents migrated to Britain from Jamaica in the 1950s.

He has campaigned on a number of issues relating to Black British history and raising awareness of the Black presence in Britain. I would highly recommend going out and buying his book, *100 Great Black Britons,* detailing the lives of Black Britons who have contributed to and shaped the country we know today.

He has also taken a keen interest in his own personal history and his links to Africa, tracing his family lineage back through the slave plantations of Jamaica, all the way to the Mandinka tribe of a village called Kédougou, in Senegal.

He is rightfully considered an expert on African and Caribbean genealogy in the UK.

And so it was that a year after I'd had my out-of-body experience holding that Black Country flag, and trying to forget all about it, that I was sent an article about Patrick Vernon and it all came rushing back.

The headline read 'Fury Over Black Country "Slave Chains" Flag'[3] with a picture of me holding the flag in front of the Dudley museum with a big grin on my face.

Patrick Vernon articulated everything, all the feelings and misgivings I'd buried deep down inside myself. In an opinion piece in our regional newspaper, the *Express and Star*, Patrick wrote:

> I find the Black Country Day logo offensive, as the foundries and factories made chains, fetters, collars, padlocks and manacles which were used on slave ships from Africa and in the plantations during slavery in the Caribbean and North America . . . If we were in America the chains logo would be seen as the equivalent of the Confederate Flag.[4]

Patrick then went on to explain that, like me, he is proud of his Black Country roots, being born in Wolverhampton, and wanted a flag that recognised the area's multicultural present.

At the very end of the piece, he referred directly to the picture of me holding up the flag whilst smiling to camera: 'I am sure if Lenny Henry was aware of this history along with the general public, we would be having a different conversation about truth and reconciliation.'

The fact is, I did know better. I just didn't know how to express it at the time.

This book is my attempt to initiate that 'different conversation'.

A conversation exploring the truths about the history of

slavery and what it means to Black people – especially those of us living in Britain. (Please note the plural on 'truths', as I believe that in any argument there are nearly always a number of truths that can be correct at the same time.)

And, of course, exploring the prospect of some kind of reconciliation, which I believe must include reparations.

So there you have it. The initiation and origin of this entire project. Me and the Black Country flag – smiling and waving on the outside whilst on the inside, wondering, 'Hang on – chains? Wait a minute!'

We live in a complicated world where Black history education is crammed into one month a year. This is probably a good time to say, 'My name is Lenny Henry and, for your information, I'm Black all year round. Would you please include Black history on all curriculums so that our children can be less ignorant about their past than I was?' This book hopes to give the reader a structure through which they can discuss issues of reparation and the history of slavery. Hope it helps.

2: BRITISH SLAVERY ENDED 1 FEBRUARY 2015

It's February 2018, four years after I held the infamous flag, and I have just discovered that *for my entire working life* I had been paying compensation to former slave owners for 'losing' the privilege to work my foremothers and forefathers into the grave.

I realised that I'd been paying a proportion of every pay cheque I'd ever received to pacify irate slave owners who were no longer allowed to benefit from exploiting, torturing and even killing people that look like me.

How did I find out about this horrific reality, you might ask?

Was it broken to me gently, accompanied by an apology? Perhaps with all the money I had paid to these slave owners returned to me with interest? Or with the kindly and sincere recognition that a terrible mistake had been made, and in fact I was the one owed compensation?

Nope.

I found out through possibly one of the most bizarre and insensitive tweets in history – and that is really saying something when you think about all the weird crazy things posted on social media.

The tweet was posted by the official account of HM Treasury, @hmtreasury, on Friday 9 February 2019. It read:

> Here's today's surprising #FridayFact. Millions of you helped end the slave trade through your taxes.

And was accompanied by an illustration of enslaved Black people, bound and shackled, walking through a tropical climate, with the caption:

> In 1833, Britain used £20 million, 40% of its national budget, to buy freedom for all slaves in the Empire. The amount of money borrowed for the Slavery Abolition Act was so large that it wasn't paid off until 2015. Which means that living British citizens helped pay to end the slave trade.

To make matters even worse, the image used of the bound and shackled Black people – the men, children and women with small babies strapped to their backs – showed them being led by other armed Black people. One Black man at the front casually carries a gun on his right shoulder and another Black man is at the back carrying his gun over his left.

Just in case this depiction of Black men, women, children and infants being forcibly ripped from their homes and marched in shackles is not enough to bring home the brutal realities of slavery for the viewer, at the left-hand side of the illustration is a man holding an axe above his head, which he is about to bring down on another man. The second, defenceless, man is on the ground with his arm raised in what is clearly a futile attempt to defend himself from the swing of the axe.

Just in case you are in any doubt, the axe wielder about to end the life of this unarmed person is, yet again, a Black man.

One final point I want to make about this image, a point I suspect most people miss. There are no buildings. The enslaved Black people who are bound and shackled, the Black people who are carrying guns, the small drama unfolding in the corner of the illustration of a Black man about to be hacked to death by another Black man, this is all against a backdrop of what one can only assume is an African wilderness. Birds fly overhead and there are trees and bushes in the foreground. There are no signs of development or architecture of any kind – just wilderness.

So there you have it. In one tweet you have the five ways that far too many people think about slavery:

1. It was brutal.
2. Africans were taken from a land that was 'uncivilised'.
3. The Black people suffered – some were even killed.
4. 'We' should be proud that we ended it.
5. 'We' don't like to think about the bad white people involved in slavery, and we definitely won't show them, let alone talk about them.

I've used the word 'we' deliberately here, because invariably the conversation is framed in terms of white people talking to other white people. This is not how this book is going to be framed.

It would be difficult to sufficiently counter all the incorrect underlying assumptions contained within the tweet and everything it got wrong in one chapter – there are literally hundreds of books dedicated to each mistake. However, in brief: West Africa, the place from which the majority of Africans were abducted, was far from 'uncivilised' when the European transatlantic slave trade started. The idea 'we' should be proud for ending slavery is questionable at best when Britain was the country that led the world in the trade. The focus on Africans enslaving their own and the effective (often subconscious) erasure of white people in the abhorrent trade is a constant phenomenon in depictions and discussions about transatlantic slavery. And the idea that Britain is still fundamentally a 'white country' is evident in the use of the word 'we'. Finally, the Treasury's tweet stated that 'millions of you helped end the slave *trade* through your taxes', and the illustration used in the tweet was of slavers and their captives. In actual fact, *trade* in slavery ended in 1807, but *slavery* in the British colonies ended thirty years later. The compensation paid in 1833 was for the end of slavery itself not the end of the trade.

But it was not these factual mistakes and erroneous assumptions that made the tweet so important. It was the bigger truth that it unveiled that made global headlines.

The backlash against the Treasury's tweet was quick, angry and incredulous.

Bristol historian Kirsten Elliott was quoted in the *Mirror* saying: 'Am I right in thinking that means that descendants of slaves – who never got any compensation – have been paying for the compensation paid to slave owners?'[1]

Historian David Olusoga, who has written extensively about Bristol's role in the slave trade, questioned why anyone in the Treasury thought the tweet was appropriate, asking: 'The real question is why anyone thought this was ok? . . . I really do think we're getting better at accepting the UK's role in slavery and the slave trade, but things like this make me question my optimism.'[2]

Other reactions on social media were less diplomatic and reserved, with one Black Briton – Lexington Wright – tweeting: 'So basically, my father and his children and grandchildren have been paying taxes to compensate those who enslaved our ancestors, and you want me to be proud of that fact. Are you f**king insane???'[3]

Within twenty-four hours the Treasury had deleted the tweet, recognising that it was ill judged.

But for me this is where the story really gets interesting.

In response to the *Bristol Post* as to why and how they decided to post the tweet in the first place, a spokesperson for the Treasury explained: 'In response to a freedom of information request, we recently published information on government expenditure related to the abolishment of slavery in 1833.'[4] The statement continued, 'An accompanying tweet was also posted, but later deleted in acknowledgement of concerns raised about the sensitivity of the subject.'

Freedom of information requests in the UK were only made possible following the Freedom of Information Act 2000, an Act of Parliament that created a statutory right for the public to request and access information held by public authorities. It was this Act that enabled someone to not only ask the Treasury one of the most important questions about British transatlantic slavery, but to actually get an answer. It is unclear who made the original Freedom of Information request but the Treasury's response in full is still available online:

> Thank you for your Freedom of Information enquiry of 5 January 2018. You asked for the following information:
>
> '". . . In 1833, Britain used 40% of its national budget to buy freedom for all slaves in the Empire. Britain borrowed such a large sum of money for the Slavery Abolition Act that it wasn't paid off until 2014. This means that living British citizens helped pay for the ending of the slave trade with their taxes."
>
> i] Is it true in 1833 Britain used 40% of its budget to buy freedom for slaves in the Empire?
>
> ii] Can you confirm that the borrowed money for the Abolition Act was only paid off in 2014?'
>
> I can confirm that HM Treasury does hold information within the scope of your request.
>
> The Government used £20 million to fund the Slavery Abolition Act 1833. In 1833, this was equivalent to approximately 40% of the Government's total annual

expenditure. This information is available online.

Information on the compensation payable under the Slavery Abolition Act 1833 can be found here: http://discovery.nationalarchives.gov.uk/details/r/C11249

Information on the UK's Budget in 1833 can be found on tab A27 of the Bank of England's 'A millennium of macroeconomic data' spreadsheet, which can be found here: https://www.bankofengland.co.uk/statistics/research-datasets

In answering your second question, it may be useful to explain how the UK Government's borrowing works. The majority of Government borrowing is financed through the issuance of UK Government bonds known as gilts by the Debt Management Office (DMO) and as such, the majority of the Government's debt is held in gilts. A gilt is a financial instrument that pays coupons (interest payments) twice per year to the holder of the gilt, up to and including the date on which the amount borrowed is finally repaid. Gilts are typically sold to large investment banks which, in turn, sell the gilts on to end-investors. These banks are known as the Gilt-Edged Market Makers and consist of 19 firms.

The Slavery Abolition Act (1835) Loan was rolled over into the Government's gilt programme, ultimately into an undated gilt, the 4% Consolidated Loan (1957 or after). The term 'undated' refers to the fact that this gilt was issued with an earliest potential redemption date of 1957, but it was not compulsory for the gilt to be redeemed at this date. The 4% Consolidated Loan was redeemed on 1 February 2015, as part of the Government's decision to modernise the gilt portfolio by redeeming all remaining undated gilts. More information about undated gilts can be found on the DMO's website here: http://www.dmo.gov.uk/responsibilities/gilt-market/about-gilts/

Money borrowed to fund the Slavery Abolition Act (1835) was therefore fully repaid in 2015. The long gap between this money being borrowed and its repayment was due to the type of financial instrument that was used, rather than the amount of money borrowed.[5]

Now, Marcus Ryder – my co-author – is a journalist and academic, and I know he loves looking at Freedom of Information requests. The best ones ask simple questions that no one has thought to ask before, seeking information that is hiding in plain sight. (I say 'plain sight' because it has to be information that the public organisation can readily retrieve. Asking a simple question can reframe the whole debate about an issue.)

This Freedom of Information request was genius, and dare I admit it, both Marcus and I were slightly jealous that we hadn't thought of asking it ourselves.

Those of us who are interested in slavery, and more specifically the abolition of slavery, already knew that the government of the day compensated the slave owners when slavery was abolished. Three years before the Freedom of Information request, David Olusoga had made an award-winning programme for the BBC titled *Britain's Forgotten Slave Owners* in which he laid this all out.[6] We already knew that the amount the British government paid out was an enormous amount of money.

But what was genius about the request was it reframed the debate in two ways:

Firstly, it put the amount of compensation the government paid not as an absolute figure (£20 million) but as a percentage of government economic activity. (Don't worry if you don't know anything about economics and government expenditure

– we'll get to that when we calculate exactly how much the Big Payback should be in Chapter 6.)

Secondly, the request was groundbreaking because the person who submitted it realised that governments don't have 40 per cent of their GDP simply lying around in a bank account, or down the back of the sofa. They have to borrow the money, and will only finish repaying it in the future. Repaying borrowed money in the future means that future taxpayers have to pay it back. And that means you and me.

All of a sudden the abolition of slavery was not something that happened almost 200 years ago, but something that, in a very concrete way, ended only less than ten years ago. That means that any Black person who has ever paid taxes to the British government before 2015 has paid compensation to the slave owners for the apparent 'privilege' of being free.

The consequence of slavery is not something that affects Black people living today in the abstract. This was one very real example of how the impact has been felt by us up until 2015.

Coincidentally, I also find it interesting that the author of this ingenious Freedom of Information request must have crunched the numbers themselves and got it slightly wrong, thinking that the debt was paid off in 2014, when in reality it was 2015. When it comes to slavery, no matter how close you might estimate the reaches of its impact to be, it invariably ends up being even closer. Something I am shocked by every day.

Once you realise the size of the compensation Britain paid out to former slave owners, and the immorality of a system that saw Black people paying money to slave owners for their own freedom, the whole discussion around slavery is reframed and the next step in the argument is almost inevitable.

After the Treasury's infamous tweet, calls for Black people

living today to be compensated for slavery came thick and fast.

Two weeks after the infamous tweet was deleted, a press conference was held 4,679 miles away in Kingston, Jamaica, by Sir Hilary Beckles, the Vice Chancellor of the University of the West Indies and the Chair of the Caribbean Community and Common Market (CARICOM) Reparations Commission.

Sir Hilary explained what the tweet really meant and its logical consequences. He pointed out that the tweet confirmed what many people already knew and felt, that far from slavery being something in the dim and distant past it was a 'present-day issue'.

He also used the new information revealed in the tweet to criticise a speech made in 2015 by the then British prime minister David Cameron during a visit to Jamaica, urging the Caribbean and all descendants of British-owned slaves to 'move on' from slavery. 'For me it is the greatest act of political immorality to be told consistently and persistently to put [slavery] in the past,' Sir Hilary said, adding, 'and yet Her Majesty's Treasury has released the relevant information to suggest that it is just two years ago that this bond was being repaid.'[7]

At the same time as Sir Hilary in Jamaica was using the information from the Freedom of Information request and the Treasury's deleted tweet to counter the idea that slavery was something that had happened ages ago and that we just need to 'move on', Cleo Lake, a Black local government councillor back in the UK, in Bristol, also seized on the tweet, announcing that she 'shared the disgust of all those who are now finding out'[8] about the issue.

Cleo Lake launched a petition with a group called the 'Global Afrikan People's Parliament' demanding that all the money that compensated the slave owners for their loss of 'property' should be paid back to British taxpayers. Writing directly to the Treasury, the petition framed the issue as 'tax fraud'[9].

It read:

> To – HM Revenue & Customs
>
> We are compelled by the dictates of our conscience to sign this petition initiated by the Global Afrikan People's Parliament, the representative body of the emergent MAATUBUNTUJAMAA Afrikan Heritage Community for National Self-Determination (AHC-NSD). We act as conscientious objectors to tax fraud. Accordingly, we demand a full refund of monies that taxpayers in Britain have unknowingly been forced by state coercion to pay in clearing the 'debt' the United Kingdom incurred by awarding unjust compensation to families that profited from the Maangamizi crimes of chattel enslavement.
>
> We share the disgust of all those who are now finding out, that for many generations, monies were extorted from all those paying taxes in Britain, right up until 2015, for the compensation that was the unjust reward legislated by the 1833 Slavery Abolition Act. By such an Act the unrepresentative parliament and state at the time rewarded those families they set up, defended and patronised, in carrying out what they saw as the lucrative 'business' of the Transatlantic Traffic in Enslaved Afrikans.
>
> The notion that we as tax payers in Britain, including those whose ancestors were subjected to the horrors of enslavement, have by your own admission, financially contributed to such payments, is totally unjust and abhorrent to us. There are peoples of conscience throughout the world who share this viewpoint of ours, more so as the British Empire extracted resources globally to fund such payments.

We at no time consented to the misuse of our tax monies to reward such abominable crimes. We therefore demand refund in full so that such funds can be put to better use in repairing the harms done and paid for not in our names. Out of such refunds an Afrikan Heritage Community Educational Trust can be established and managed with strict community accountability as a contribution to repairing such harms and their continuing legacies.

It was, of course, no coincidence that Ms Lake was a councillor in the city that hosts one of the few British museums dedicated to the transatlantic slave trade. Bristol officially became involved in the transatlantic trade in enslaved Africans in 1698, and, according to the museum, 'By the late 1730s Bristol had become Britain's premier slaving port. In 1750 alone, Bristol ships transported some 8,000 of the 20,000 enslaved Africans sent that year to the British Caribbean and North America.' According to some estimates, up until the abolition of the slave trade, half a million enslaved Africans passed through the port city. It is almost impossible to look around the city and not see evidence of the slavery, as profits from the trade went into funding landmarks including the Clifton Suspension Bridge, Bristol Cathedral's stained-glass windows, and Bristol University's main Wills Memorial Building.

British slave owners who were compensated for the abolition of slavery would have included many of Bristol's richest businessmen and women who owned vast plantations in the Caribbean and North America, as well as thousands of 'regular' Bristolians who profited from the trade.

Cleo Lake, like Sir Hilary, recognised that the Treasury's tweet put paid to the lie that the transatlantic slave trade was something that happened in the dim and distant past and something that we all had to 'move on' from. The repercussions of the slave trade are still very much with us, and the idea of who should be compensated is still a live issue – especially as repayments only finished a few years earlier.

That one deleted tweet resonated around the world; it was reported across Africa, Europe, America and even Asia.

The Treasury may have seen it as a mistake and deleted it within hours of posting. But personally, I think it is one of the most important tweets in the history of social media.

It brought the issue of who should be compensated for the ending of the horrors of transatlantic slavery up to date and to a global audience.

Whether the Treasury meant to or not – and I am pretty sure they did not mean to – the issue of reparations has now become one that we all have to think about.

The next question is, 'What exactly are reparations?'

3: HUMPTY DUMPTY'S PROBLEM WITH DEFINITIONS

Although most people know me for my work on stage and in front of the camera, as a comedian and actor, I don't think I am being immodest when I say that, over the last ten years, Marcus Ryder and I have been leading voices in the UK media industry when it comes to diversity.

Back in 2014, Marcus and I, with a team of Black media professionals, crafted a speech I then delivered at the British Academy Film Awards which changed the way people talk about diversity in film and TV. It was part of what BAFTA call their 'Gurus' lecture series – a title which to me felt a bit much, to be honest. Yes, it was difficult to write and we did give it a lot of thought, but none of us had been sitting cross-legged on top of a mountain next to a goat for a decade in quiet contemplation. Nonetheless the speech was a turning point in the UK media industry.

Then, in 2016, Marcus and I successfully lobbied for the term 'diversity' to be included in the BBC's royal charter for the first time in its hundred-year history. From that point onwards the BBC has had to include diversity in everything it does in order to meet its obligations to the UK government.

In 2018, with other famous actors and TV personalities including Meera Syal, Adrian Lester and Ade Adepitan, we marched on 10 Downing Street to demand that the government implement diversity tax breaks for film and TV productions. This proposal asserted that film and TV productions that reached a certain diversity threshold in employing women, disabled and people of colour, would be eligible for extra tax relief on top of the existing compensation for films and high-end TV produced in the UK.

Truth be told, we didn't quite march – it was more of a saunter. Yes! We sauntered up the famous street giving interviews as we walked. Marcus's mum was there to wave – and even gave him a boiled egg in case he got hungry. But I digress . . . I am trying to point out how, together, Marcus and I have been at the forefront of a campaign to increase diversity in film and TV.

Most recently, in 2020 we launched the Sir Lenny Henry Centre for Media Diversity at Birmingham City University to work with major media organisations, from the liberal/left Channel 4 to the Piers Morgan-friendly News UK, to support them with their diversity efforts. And yes, I admit naming the Centre after myself is a bit much, but for the record, your honour, it wasn't my choice.

In 2021 we even wrote a book about our adventures in diversity and equality (*Access All Areas: The Diversity Manifesto for TV and Beyond*). I say all this not because I like to show off (who doesn't?) but as you'll know if you've read that book, there was one important – painful – lesson I learnt in doing all this work to support diversity: you need to define your terms.

In *Access All Areas*, Marcus and I wrote a whole chapter titled 'Humpty Dumpty Sat on a Wall . . .' This bit of the book was all about the fact that, while people may like the idea of diversity, a key challenge in achieving it is that the word 'diversity' can literally mean anything anybody wants it to mean. We called it the 'Humpty Dumpty problem', named after the famous exchange in Lewis Carroll's *Alice's Adventures in Wonderland* between Humpty Dumpty and Alice:

HUMPTY DUMPTY'S PROBLEM

'When *I* use a word,' Humpty Dumpty said, in rather a scornful tone, 'it means just what I choose it to mean – neither more nor less.'

'The question is,' said Alice, 'whether you *can* make words mean so many different things.'

'The question is,' said Humpty Dumpty, 'which is to be master – that's all.'

Not properly defining 'diversity' at the beginning of our campaigning meant that in the real world, all our hard work made little difference; organisations just defined it however they wanted – set their own homework, assessed it, marked it, deemed it satisfactory and then declared, 'Hell yeah baby! We diverse!' It's a crucial lesson for all advocacy and campaign work.

I was not going to make the same mistake twice when it came to reparations. And so I spoke to Marcus and he said he had the perfect solution . . .

'Let's google it!'

According to the first dictionary definition that came up on my Google search, 'reparations are help or payment that someone gives another person for damage, loss or suffering that they have caused that other person'.

'And in this case,' Marcus pointed out, 'we are talking about payment to Black people for slavery and colonialism.' Humpty Dumpty solved!

I didn't bother to point out that if I believed everything on Google, I'd be presenting *News at Ten* and aliens would have been living peacefully in the Lake District since the sixties whilst quietly taking over the rest of the world – which is flat, by the way.

But I did say that we should keep thinking about the Humpty Dumpty problem.

It just so happened that, at the time, we were in the middle of recording a podcast series based on another book we co-edited, *Black British Lives Matter: A Clarion Call for Equality*. (Wanna buy one? I've got a garage full of 'em!)

So Marcus's second suggestion was that we do a podcast episode on reparations and ask one of the leading voices on reparations in the UK to define it for us.

Esther Stanford-Xosei was born in South London to Caribbean parents, and has direct ancestral links to the victims of the transatlantic slave trade. She describes herself as a 'guerrilla lawyer' specialising in 'applied jurisprudence, the science, philosophy and study of law through its actual practice'[1].

She seems to be part of more organisations involved in reparations than the Wakandan inner council, including, but definitely not limited to: the Pan-Afrikan Reparations Coalition in Europe, Stop the Maangamizi Campaign, Global Afrikan People's Parliament, and the International Network of Scholars and Activists for Afrikan Reparations.

Marcus knew she was the best person to talk to about reparations in the UK, that she would give us a strong foundational understanding of what reparations actually are and, most importantly, what they are not – cutting through the misunderstandings, half-truths and stereotypes.

If anyone was going to solve our Humpty Dumpty/reparations problem, it was going to be Esther. Our pre-Zoom chat was a touch intimidating. On first impressions, she seemed like the kind of person who does not suffer fools and has an urgency when it comes to the matter of achieving reparations that is almost visceral.

But the first lesson she taught me on reparations happened even before she stepped into the virtual podcast recording studio. When she was first asked to appear on our podcast, her reaction to Marcus's invitation was a polite but firm, 'No, thank you.'

It turned out that the title of the podcast was the problem.

The podcast was to support the book *Black British Lives Matter* and so for each episode our idea was to discuss a different issue, inserting the name of the issue into the title of the book. So, for example, we did one episode titled 'Black British Mental Health Matters' another one called 'Black British Music Matters', and so on.

This episode was naturally called 'Black British Reparations Matter'. To us it seemed innocuous enough, but Esther was NOT happy.

She politely explained why: 'There is no such thing as a Black British reparations movement.' She feared what we were trying to do with the podcast was to separate Black British people from Black people living in Africa, the Caribbean and the rest of the world. She explained, 'There's never been a solely Black British movement when it comes to reparations and that's largely because our origins come from outside of the UK. We can trace direct family connections to parts of the Caribbean, other parts of the Americas and certainly Africa.'

She was particularly critical of campaigners in the US who argue that reparations should go to only 'African Americans' – people with direct links to their family being enslaved in North America. She thought we were trying to do the same thing, but in a British context.

In her words: 'When we think about reparations we need to think globally, even if I come to the issue as a Black Briton.'

Once we'd changed the title of the podcast to 'Reparations Matter', Esther agreed to participate, and I learnt that any definition of reparations must be global. That was the first part of the definition.

When she took her place at the mic, I posed the question I'd been dying to ask:

'Esther, according to the dictionary – reparations are "help or payment that someone gives another person for damage, loss or suffering that they have caused that other person", but what's your definition of reparations?'

After a deep breath she started:

'So, reparations as a concept is one of the most misunderstood terms, with obviously popular understandings of it associating reparations with financial compensation, or money repayments. However, the root of the word "reparation" is from the Latin *reparare*, which basically means to repair harm.'

I was suddenly eight years old again. I was making that Scooby Doo face. Huh? She saw this and tried to break it down.

'If you look at the English dictionary definition of 'repair', there are two meanings. One of the meanings speaks to the fact that whatever is to be repaired, has been harmed – in this case we are talking about people; there must be a reparations process that brings about transformation of that particular people or group or individual that has been harmed.'

She hadn't even got to the second definition at this point but I knew I was in safe hands; Marcus had found the right person to start our reparations journey.

Having begun in a way that an eight-year-old would understand, she then took it up a gear:

'So in the reparations movement that I'm part of, known as the International Social Movement for African Reparations, we use two main frameworks . . .'

(When I first discussed writing this book to my publishers, they asked me who I thought this book would appeal to. And I responded, 'Everyone interested in racism, the legacy of slavery and reparations.' And the editor looked at me and replied, 'Everyone?' And then he looked at Marcus and asked, 'It's not going to be too nerdy, is it?'

So here is my dilemma: to really understand the issues behind reparations we need to speak to the academics, you know who I'm talkin' about: the 'nerds'!

So, this next bit we'll have to 'de-nerdify' and paraphrase. Bear with.)

According to Esther the first framework they use to define reparations was developed by the mononymous academic Chinweizu at the First Conference on Reparations for Enslavement, Colonisation and Neo-colonialism, in Nigeria in 1993.

According to Chinweizu's definition, reparations are mostly about making repairs. And here's the kicker: the focus is not on what white people – or the descendants of slave owners – should give us as Black people. The focus should be on 'self-made' repairs on ourselves.

Esther explained patiently, 'So even if there are monies – the focus is on us being in the driving seat of determining what those repairs are.'

This means that Chinweizu looks at the damage done to Black people psychologically, culturally, socially, economically, politically, educationally, and asks the question, 'What do we need in order to recreate and sustain healthy Black societies?' And in his analysis, far more important than any monies associated with any reparations process is the *opportunity and space for Black people to repair ourselves*; the opportunity for us to rehabilitate our minds, our material condition, our collective reputation, our collective cultural memories, our self-respect, our religious and political traditions and our family institutions.

He argues that all of these things were destroyed by the transatlantic slave trade, and we have still not been given the opportunity – due to racism and other factors – to repair this damage.

According to Esther, when it comes to reparations, 'first and foremost it's the rehabilitation of our mind – that colonial mind – that has been impacted by enslavement. Repairing that is at the centre of the first definition of reparations.'

Now, dear reader, if you are anything like me and have had to read that a few times to try and make sense of it, let me explain what I make of that definition.

I think it can be summed up in one line written by the great Jamaican poet Robert Nesta Marley in 'Redemption Song': 'Emancipate yourselves from mental slavery. None but ourselves can free our minds.'

Reparations is not about money, or, at least, money should not be the main focus. The primary focus must be psychological and Black people must be in the driving seat. We can't be waiting for someone else to solve our problems and give us a big handout.

Listening to Esther made sense, but did that really mean that we weren't owed any money for all the unpaid work our ancestors had done during slavery? Did I really just need to think myself better? I am pretty sure the former slave owners, when they received their reparation cheques for having to give up their slaves, did not turn around and say, 'No thank you, take your paltry cash payout, I will just work on my psychological well-being.'

But I should have been more patient. Esther had said there were *two* definitions of reparations, and she had only outlined the first one.

I was hoping the second one would have a large pay cheque at the end of it. I listened intently.

'Now the second definition is known as the "operational framework on reparations", which is the framework of reparations under international law that was codified in 2005. It's called (take a deep breath): "the basic principles and guidelines on the right to a remedy and reparation for victims of violations of international human rights law and international humanitarian law". And these principles have been developed over centuries,' Esther explained. 'In fact, the principle of reparations goes back to the mandate charter of the Mandinka people going back to 1222.'

Now this was a definition I could warm to. Recognised by international law and with roots going back to Africa. (The Mandinka people are a West African ethnic group primarily found in southern Mali, Gambia, southern Senegal and eastern Guinea. Yes, I'm all about Google too.)

Then Esther slowly explained this second definition:

'The contemporary international law framework has five key strands. So any reparations programme or settlement or policy must embrace these five aspects. So the five principles very quickly are . . .' Now I love Esther, but lemme paraphrase:

One: cessation of violations. The first part of reparations is making sure the original crime has stopped.

Two: assurances and guarantees of non-repetition. Which means, once the original crime has stopped, ensuring that what has happened to a people who have been harmed – in this case the transatlantic slave trade – never happens again.

Three: the idea of restitution – this broadly means, to put the people who have been wronged *back* in the position that they might have occupied, had they not been enslaved. In other words, if the transatlantic slave trade hadn't happened, where would the descendants of those enslaved Africans be today? And what would they be doing?

Four: the notion of compensation, though not just about money, includes putting an economic value on harm. When it comes to the transatlantic slave trade, that value is not just reflective of the harm of not paying my ancestors for all the unpaid work they did but also about *compensation* for all the harm inflicted on those who experienced slavery and any ongoing harm due to its legacy.

And finally five: the notion of *satisfaction*. Now this is a really interesting one. Esther called this 'symbolic reparations'. It covers things such as rewriting the national history, changing street names, pulling down public statutes of former slave owners like Edward Colston. In her words, 'It's those symbolic measures that a society undertakes to demonstrate that it has really grappled with the harm that has been inflicted on a particular group and has sought to change the way that group is viewed in society by teaching the truth about their history.'

After she'd outlined the five basic tenets behind this second definition of reparations, Esther went on to explain one more crucial thing.

'When we define reparations, one aspect that doesn't get emphasised enough is the idea that we are basically rehabilitating people individually, families and communities. A lot of us have found ways to cope with the consequences of the harm that has been inflicted on past generations – not to mention the ongoing harm – and we've developed some behaviour patterns that get passed on intergenerationally that are not serving us.'

These five points, and especially that last additional one,

literally blew my mind; she then began to propose a road map – to end racism for ever.

Reparations isn't just about the cheque – although let's not forget point four: compensation. (Could a massive cheque be coming my way? Lovely if true, but more on that in Chapter 9.) Reparations is about truly repairing the harm that has resulted from the transatlantic slave trade, and surely one of the biggest harms created by slave trade is the foundation and endurance of racism. The notion that one race is superior to another.

Esther had joined our podcast, settled in to bat and immediately scored a six with the first ball, helping us avoid that tricksy Humpty Dumpty problem.

Now, I should also mention that we had one other guest on the podcast that day, Kehinde Andrews. One of the coolest and smartest professors you will ever meet. He launched the first Black Studies degree in Europe, and has written more books on race, racism, slavery and colonialism than I've had hot dinners. (I've had nuff hot dinners.)

Although Esther had just given the most comprehensive definition of reparations ever, I asked Kehinde to define the idea as well.

His interpretation was far less technical but emotionally it hit a lot harder:

'I always go to Malcolm X, because, you know, why not? Why go to anyone else? Right?' he started, in his slow, smoother-than-a-cat-wearing-a-velvet-tuxedo manner.

'And Malcolm says that if you stick a knife in my back nine inches, and you only pull it out six inches, well, that's not progress, right? Even if you pull it all the way out, that's still not progress, *you have to heal the wound*, right? And that's what reparations is really about.'

'Reparations is saying, there's damage that has been done, and it needs to be healed. And if it's not healed, have we really made any progress?'

Clearly, Marcus and I did not want to make the same mistake we'd made with diversity. We had our definition. But even having helped Humpty Dumpty find the master, we still had a long way to go. In particular, we had to know whether reparations really could heal the huge wound of the transatlantic slave trade. *Could reparations cure racism?*

4: THE END OF RACISM

Could reparations end racism?

I remember watching in 2020 the Black Lives Matter marches around the world and it felt as if the whole world had shifted. From Kazakhstan to Brazil, from Düsseldorf to Dudley – millions of folks were out there marching against racism. Almost everyone, whatever colour they were, protested to end discrimination against the descendants of the transatlantic slave trade. People who look like George Floyd. People who look like me.

The England football team took the knee before they played their matches in recognition of the racism that exists in society. VAR checked it, made 'em do it again.

In the world of British television, a variety of efforts were made by broadcasters in response to the demonstrations and, of course, the death of George Floyd.

Sky committed £30 million 'to support the fight against racial injustice and invest more in diversity and inclusion'.[1]

The BBC, not to be outdone, ring-fenced £112 million over three years for 'diverse' productions.[2]

And while Channel 4 might not have access to the same amount of money as Sky or the BBC, they responded to the global clarion call to end racism by putting on an entire day of programmes featuring just Black people in front of the camera and as many Black people as they could find to work behind the camera.

For my part, I edited a collection of essays with Marcus titled *Black British Lives Matter*.

We were going to end racism.

Spoiler alert: as we're writing this in 2024, racism is gaining momentum. Far-right political parties are stronger than ever across Europe. In the UK, the Reform Party has four seats in parliament – something they did not have before we attempted to 'end racism' in 2020 (I am definitely *not* saying Nigel Farage and followers are a racist party, but I would just point out that when a party has to expel prospective parliamentary candidates for calling Rishi Sunak a f**king P*k*, it would seem racists may very well have been attracted to that party).

What one friend disparagingly termed 'Black Square Summer' – due to all the social media posts professing support for Black Lives Matter and vowing to end racism – has turned into an ongoing 'Cold White Winter' less than four years later.

Nevertheless, I do think the goals of the protests in 2020 remain admirable ones. I still want Black lives to matter and be valued. And I still want to end racism.

Specifically, if one of the five key points or definitions of racism is – as Esther Stanford-Xosei articulately outlined in the last chapter – the notion of restitution, to put a people or a group back in the position that they would have been in, but for what has happened to them, then reparations may well be the answer to ending racism after all.

Bear with me as I present a little story about a Black boy growing up in Dudley in the UK in the 1960s.

When I was a kid, I lived quite an isolated experience in what was, to all intents and purposes, a Jamaican household – where people spoke with a Jamaican accent, ate Jamaican food, and argued about Jamaican politics. But I was definitely not in Jamaica – I was in Dudley in the West Midlands of England. And when I went out into the world, I was Black. I might have had a broad Dudley accent and I definitely had white friends, but I was acutely aware that I was different.

My mum, a strict Jamaican matriarch with size-twelve feet and biceps like Popeye, told us one day that we had to 'h'integrate!' with the Dudley people dem, or we 'wouldn't fit in!' I did this – or at least tried to. At school, there was this one kid (let's call him Nigel) who picked on me every day. As soon as I arrived at the school gates, I'd be racially abused and then Nigel and I would roll around on the floor, punching, kicking, biting, surrounded by a feral crowd of schoolkids baying for blood. During this, Nigel would yell words such as 'coon', 'wog', 'nig nog' – all the hits, all the time. Afterwards, I'd just stagger off to class, bruised both externally and internally. Then one day, I had an epiphany. I got to school and immediately Nigel began his mantra: 'Henry! Y' just a coon', 'wog', 'darky', 'spade' and the rest – and we began the whole rolling-around-in-the-dirt scenario. Then a light bulb appeared above my head – and I said this: 'Nigel, you must really fancy me cos we're always rolling around on the floor with each other.' And then, I heard the best noise of all time – a raucous laugh from the kids who were standing around watching us fight. I doubled down, 'Why don't we just pick out a ring and make it official?' A bigger laugh. This was great! 'Where d'you wanna go on our honeymoon?' Nigel hit me a few more times but, as my attempts at late-twentieth-century metrosexual material met with even more laughter, Nigel ran out of steam and muttered to himself – 'Are we gonna fight or what?' and then wandered off.

I had refused to stoop to his level. I'd done something much better than fighting. I'd discovered that humour could be my sword and my shield against racism. Don't get me wrong, after my epiphany moment, Nigel still bullied me and called me names, but the violent incidents of this behaviour began to lessen until he eventually left me alone.

All of this was brought home to me when I was just eleven years old. A good time to learn that the pen is mightier than the sword and also that a weird conversational diversion can confuse the hell out of a kid that's got you in a headlock. Comedy rocks.

OK. I know what you're thinking: 'Yes, racism is bad. Yes, I am sure nearly every Black Briton has a story like this. But what has this got to do with reparations and the transatlantic slave trade?' Now, Nigel might have been a little racist. But he is not a slave owner and I am not a slave. So how do I think reparations will solve racism? It all comes back to that third point in the definition of reparations: *'putting a people or a group back in the position that they would have been in, but for what has happened to them.'*

◆

I believe the reason we have racism today and also

- why people from Black African backgrounds in the UK typically hold the least wealth, less than one-eighth of the wealth held by white British people;[3]
- why Black British people are twice as likely to be unemployed as their white counterparts;[4]
- why Black British people are grossly over-represented in the prison population (seven times, to be precise, according to one study)[5]

is all because of the transatlantic slave trade.

And fixing the harm caused by the transatlantic slave trade is the only way to solve racism. Point three of the definition is everything.

I don't believe people are born racist.

I don't believe the children who were racist to me at school were born racist. But more to the point, I don't believe their parents — or even the majority of adults in that case — are clever enough (or stupid enough) to generate the sheer tonnage of racial prejudice we have today.

When you take a step back, and think about it objectively, discriminating against people on the basis of their skin colour makes as much sense as hating someone because of their shoe size, or the colour of their eyes.

Racism is not a natural phenomenon. Genetic differences might be natural but classifying these genetic differences into different races and then privileging some people and discriminating against others on the basis of it is not natural. And it is all due to the ongoing legacy of the transatlantic slave trade.

Marcus is now gonna take the reins for a little history lesson. I want you to give a warm hand to my deejay and co-conspirator. Count it off — one, two, three, four — hit it!

◆

Marcus: Thanks, Len. Here's a quick overview of how the ideas of different races and racism were created. For longer explanations I would heavily recommend reading *The Myth of Race: The Troubling Persistence of an Unscientific Idea* by Robert Wald Sussman, *Superior: The Return of Race Science* by Angela Saini and *The Origin of Races and Color* by Martin R. Delany, a classic originally published in 1879.

How the Ideas of Different Races and Racism Were Created

The concept of race is a relatively modern construct, with its origins deeply intertwined with European colonialism and the transatlantic slave trade. While human societies have always recognised differences among groups based on physical appearance, language and culture, the systematic categorisation of people into races with associated hierarchical values didn't really emerge until the sixteenth century. This is when the transatlantic slave trade started.

It is commonly accepted that 1526 is the year the Portuguese completed the first transatlantic slave voyage to Brazil, with other Europeans soon following their example.

The slave trade was a huge – 'positive' – disruption to European economies. A completely new way of ordering society and extracting labour for free from entire populations.

But as much as it was a disruption to economies, it was also a disruption to society. The European population and the powers carrying it out needed a justification – they needed racism.

Racism is not a by-product of the idea of racial difference as some people think. The causality actually runs the other way round. The idea of different races is a product of racism, and racism was needed to give the transatlantic slave trade a logical underpinning.

Let me explain . . .

Prior to the modern era in Europe, distinctions among human groups were primarily based on tribal, ethnic or religious identities rather than notions of race; it is questionable whether the notion of race as we understand it today even existed.

Ancient civilisations such as the Greeks and Romans recognised differences among peoples but did not attribute these differences to immutable, hierarchical racial categories. For example, the Greeks distinguished between themselves and 'barbarians', but this was more a cultural than a racial distinction. Similarly, slavery was widespread and commonly practised in Ancient Rome, but slaves in that period were from all different ethnic groups and were not enslaved because of their ethnic affiliation. Emma Dench, a prominent classicist at Harvard University, neatly sums it up by saying it was 'notoriously difficult to detect slaves by their appearance' in Ancient Rome.[6]

Fast-forward a millennia to Medieval Europe, where people had begun categorising people largely based on religion – with Jews, Christians and Muslims seen as distinct groups.

It is not so much that people in antiquity and Medieval Europe 'didn't see colour' – the common cry of the white liberal today – but people were less likely to be categorised solely by colour, and colour was definitely not categorised in the same racial ways it is today.[7]

The turning point, and the development of the idea of race, can be directly traced to the period of European slavery and colonisation. European colonisers and settlers often described the indigenous people they encountered in terms that emphasised their supposed inferiority. This was largely driven by the need to justify the exploitation and colonisation of these peoples and their lands.

Early accounts by explorers like Christopher Columbus and subsequent settlers depicted Native Americans and Africans as 'savage' or 'primitive', laying the groundwork for racial classifications.

It was impossible to justify the crimes against humanity that were committed against entire populations without those populations first being dehumanised. And so a racial hierarchy had to be created in order to justify why one group of humans deserved to be enslaved and another group deserved to be their enslavers.

The justification for enslaving Africans was deeply intertwined with the emerging concept of race. Europeans portrayed Africans as inherently suited for hard labour and incapable of higher intellectual achievements. This degrading rhetoric was essential for rationalising the inhumane conditions and brutal treatment that enslaved Africans endured. Every part of society was then mobilised to support this emerging idea of racism. The belief in African inferiority slowly became reinforced by religious, economic and pseudoscientific arguments.

Religious justification played a significant role in the early stages of the slave trade. European colonisers often invoked the Bible to legitimise slavery, citing passages that they interpreted as endorsing the subjugation of Africans. The 'curse of Ham' from the Book of Genesis was particularly influential; according to this interpretation, Ham's descendants (believed to be Africans) were condemned to servitude.

Pseudoscientific theories further cemented the racial justification for slavery. As scientific racism gained prominence, it provided a veneer of legitimacy to the brutal exploitation of African slaves. Theories that depicted Africans as biologically inferior and suited only for manual labour were widely propagated and accepted in European and American societies.

But this was only the beginning.

By the eighteenth century, Europe entered the age of Enlightenment. The Enlightenment's emphasis on reason and science provided an even more engaging framework for understanding human differences. While racism and racial categorisation emerged to justify the enslavement of Africans in the sixteenth century, it was supercharged by thinkers such as Carl Linnaeus and Johann Friedrich Blumenbach who put a scientific spin on things. These 'thinkers' began to classify humans into different races based on physical characteristics such as skin colour, skull shape and hair texture. Linnaeus, in his seminal work *Systema Naturae* (1735), categorised humans into four varieties: Europeans, Asians, Americans and Africans, each associated with particular traits and temperaments.

Blumenbach further developed these ideas from the 1770s in works such as *On the Natural Varieties of Mankind*, proposing five human races: Caucasian, Mongolian, Malayan, Ethiopian and American. He introduced the term 'Caucasian' to describe white Europeans, suggesting that the Caucasus region was the origin of this supposedly superior race. These early attempts at scientific racial classifications were imbued with hierarchical notions, with Europeans placed at the top of the hierarchy.

Scientific racism – the use of scientific methods to justify racial differences and hierarchies – gained traction in the nineteenth century. Scientists like Samuel Morton and Josiah Nott used craniometry and other pseudoscientific methods to argue for the intellectual and moral superiority of the white race. These ideas were widely accepted and used to legitimise social and economic inequalities, primary of which was to justify the transatlantic slave trade.

The racial ideologies that emerged during this period helped to assuage any moral qualms by framing slavery of African people as a natural and beneficial arrangement for both masters and slaves.

And the legacy of those ideologies, developed specifically to justify and continue to justify the transatlantic slave trade for hundreds of years, are still with us today.

◆

Lenny: Wow. That was deep, like if the Mariana Trench had a basement. Deeper than deep. Thank you, Marcus, for that very quick and potted history of the origins of racism.

For me the killer line is the last one. We are still living with the consequences of the thinking behind the transatlantic slave trade.

There is no doubt in my mind that the racial justification for the transatlantic slave trade has had profound and lasting impact on societies across the world. The kids at my school who called me racist names. The racism my mother encountered when she came to the UK from Jamaica. Even the institutional racism in some police forces. All of these are directly related to the transatlantic slave trade. The people being racist today might not know anything about the transatlantic slave trade. But if it wasn't for the transatlantic slave trade they wouldn't even think about discriminating against Black people because of our so-called race.

Because I believe that, I also believe that we cannot end racism unless we properly address its root cause. The struggle for racial equality and justice remains a significant issue, rooted in the historical injustices of the transatlantic slave trade. That's right, people! I said the words 'transatlantic slave trade' again!

The question remains, however: how can reparations return us to a non-racist society? How can reparations help us become a post-racism society? And finally – how many more times can we mention the phrase 'transatlantic slave trade' in this chapter?

5: WHAT DID SLAVERY EVER DO FOR US?

Our professions and education clearly shape the lens through which we see the world and how we analyse things.

Marcus, for example, trained as an economist but went into television documentary making. Invariably, then, when we're discussing an issue he'll frame the problem in terms of economics and when we're structuring a book he leans heavily towards a documentarian's structure.

It's only natural, we use the tools we know.

Similarly, I've been telling jokes on stage and television since the age of sixteen, and from 1984 onwards I had numerous prime-time comedy series on BBC One.

It is impossible to go through that experience and not look at the world in terms of jokes and comedy. The best jokes often work by subverting the accepted narrative and giving you an insight into an aspect of society that we often take for granted. Looking at old jokes and routines can be a way of discovering new insights on age-old topics and I sometimes turn to them for new perspectives on ideas I'm working on.

Here is my example of using a classic sketch to better understand the transatlantic slave trade.

One of my favourite films is *Monty Python's Life of Brian*, a very silly film about a man born next door to Jesus, and on the same day, and how he gets mistaken for the Messiah.

In the film there's a scene that, like so many *Monty Python* jokes, has entered the general culture and is frequently used to understand and illustrate so much about the world.

The joke is: 'What did the Romans ever do for us?'

In the scene, a group of Jewish rebels plot against the Roman Empire, and their leader, Reg, rhetorically asks this question, 'What did the Romans ever do for us?', to emphasise their oppression. However, his question backfires as the group members start listing numerous contributions by the Romans, such as: aqueducts, sanitation, roads, irrigation, medicine, wine, public baths and public order.

For me the joke provides the perfect lens for when people talk about the transatlantic slave trade or try to say it wasn't that important.

Like the Romans in the *Life of Brian* skit, modern society and European wealth is literally built on the foundations of slavery. It is impossible to discuss reparations and not acknowledge the debt modern society, and Britain specifically, owes to the transatlantic slave trade.

And so, my remix of the *Life of Brian* joke is: 'What did slavery ever do for us?'

Marcus: Not sure about the use of the word 'us' here, maybe you should change it to 'What did the transatlantic slave trade between 1640 and 1807, followed by unfair trading practices, do for the British economy?'

Lenny: (And now you can see why I don't let Marcus loose on any of the humour. But he definitely serves his purposes in other ways.)

So, Marcus, take it away: 'What did the transatlantic slave trade between 1640 and 1807, followed by unfair trading practices, do for the British economy?'

Marcus: OK, before I get going and answer your rhetorical question in any detail, I need to start by stating that the following section draws heavily on two classic pieces of work that I would recommend everyone reads: *Capitalism and Slavery* by the great Eric Williams, and *How Europe Underdeveloped Africa* by the equally amazing Walter Rodney.

I first read *How Europe Underdeveloped Africa* when I was a teenager and it literally changed my entire world view, and I wish I'd read *Capitalism and Slavery* earlier as then I might have actually got a first in my economics degree.

But here goes . . .

Looking at What Slavery Gave Britain

Although I am going to primarily talk about economics (it is my safe space), the contribution that the transatlantic slave trade made to Britain goes far deeper and wider than just economics – from the monarchy, to banking and museums.

But before I begin, it is worth noting that while the UK gained a lot from slavery, Britain was *behind* others in trading Africans.

Britain was not the first

As we stated in the previous chapter, historians generally agree that the trade started in 1526, when a Portuguese ship completed the first transatlantic slave voyage to Brazil.

Some historians go even further back to 1441 when two Portuguese explorers, Nuno Tristão and Antam Gonçalvez, sailed to what is now Mauritania in West Africa and kidnapped twelve Africans. The captured Africans were presented as gifts to Prince Henry the Navigator back in Portugal.

But whether it's 1441 or 1526, what can be observed through records is a steady flow of enslaved Africans being taken to Spain and Portugal over that eighty-odd-year period. What started as a trickle became a steady flow and by 1500, Portugal and Spain had taken about 50,000 West Africans, mainly for working in agriculture and as domestic servants, with just a few working in sugar plantations. These sugar plantations were not in the Americas but on the Azores, Madeira, Canaries, and the Cape Verde islands.

In many ways this practice of slavery is close to the type of slavery that the world has seen dating back millennia – where slaves were used in the society their captors were from.

However, the real turning point was 1526, when the trade became 'triangular' – that is, slaves were taken to other locations and societies that the captors were not necessarily from or part of.

This point was soon after Christopher Columbus had 'discovered' the Americas in 1492 (or, as Walter Rodney puts it, 'invaded' the Americas) and in 1526 a Portuguese ship took a hundred enslaved Africans to what is now Georgetown, South Carolina.[1] That first endeavour ended in complete disaster for the Portuguese – with the African slaves rebelling, setting fire to one of the Portuguese leaders' new houses, killing the leader and then escaping.

I love this story because it shows that Africans resisted transatlantic slavery from its very inception. But the wider point is that this was the start of a different type of slavery than the world had ever seen before: taking people thousands of miles away from their home with the intention of establishing or selling those people into a society containing just enslaved people and slave owners on the basis of their race.

The other point is that, for various reasons we don't have time to explain here (another journalist, Howard French, explains very well why in his book, *Born in Blackness*), all of this was initially broadly a Spanish and Portuguese venture.

So when did Britain get involved, and why?

Slavery gave us the monarchy

Britain really only got involved in the 1600s, when some historians have argued that it was turboboosted due to the re-establishment of the English monarchy (after Oliver Cromwell) in 1685.

The new king, Charles II, ascended to the throne with the royal court in serious financial difficulty. Looking for ways to shore up his financial health and that of the people around him, the King decided to grant a royal charter to a new company, the Company of Royal Adventurers Trading in Africa. This charter gave the company exclusive rights to take part in this burgeoning new trade in enslaved Africans. It meant that no other company in Britain could compete with it and that, in return, *any profits it made would be shared between its owners and the British monarchy.*

The Company itself lasted less than twelve years, but it did successfully contribute to the stability of the British royal family, after what was a very uncertain time.

It then set the model for the Royal African Company, with James II as its governor. The Royal African Company brought considerable profits and wealth to the Crown, over its time *transporting more than 100,000 enslaved Africans from Africa to the Caribbean.*

The fact is, while we take the existence of the royal family as being a constant, unwavering feature of British society, in the 1600s its future was very uncertain and the transatlantic slave trade was central to ensuring its existence, as the monarchy itself benefited immensely from the trade.

I mention this little historical anecdote not because I am an anti-royalist . . .

(**Lenny:** Behave, I've got a knighthood bruv!)

. . . but because I think it is important if we are to answer the rhetorical *Monty Python* question, 'What did the transatlantic slave trade ever do for us?' It's easy to argue that it gave us – or, at least maintained – the royal family.

But what else?

Slavery gave us globalisation

While trade between countries is millennia old, in many ways the transatlantic slave trade created the model for economic globalisation as we know it today.

As I already mentioned, the transatlantic slave trade was different from any form of slavery the world had ever seen before. It was an entirely new way of structuring society and our idea of the world.

The transatlantic slave trade operated through a system known as the triangular trade, connecting Europe, Africa and the Americas. British ships would depart from ports like Liverpool, Bristol and London, laden with manufactured goods such as textiles, rum and guns. These goods were traded in Africa for enslaved people, who were then transported across the Atlantic to the Americas in a journey known as the Middle Passage. In the Americas, the enslaved Africans were then sold, and the proceeds were used to purchase raw materials like sugar, tobacco and cotton, which were shipped back to Britain.

Britain's involvement in the slave trade, spanning from the sixteenth to the nineteenth centuries, was a pivotal factor in the development of the British economy. It was dependent on the kidnapping, enslavement and forced labour of people from Africa. Africans were forced to work on plantations, primarily in the Caribbean and the American South, producing commodities that were in high demand in Europe. The labour of these people was crucial to the profitability of these plantations, and by extension, the British economy, and, in so doing, created an interdependent world order – that still heavily shapes the global economy today.

The profits from these plantations and the transatlantic slave trade, as well as the taxes Britain derived from them, directly, and indirectly, impacted almost every economic activity in Britain, leading it to become a world power.

Slavery gave us roads and canals

The cultivation of sugar and tobacco in the Caribbean and the American colonies played a significant role in the British economy. Sugar, often referred to as 'white gold', was particularly profitable. It was a highly sought-after commodity in Europe, used not only as a sweetener but also in the production of rum.

Tobacco was another lucrative crop, cultivated primarily in the American colonies. The high demand for tobacco in Europe created a booming industry.

The profits from sugar and tobacco plantations, completely dependent on slave labour, were immense. Importantly, the profits from these plantations in the Caribbean were reinvested in Britain. And it was this reinvestment that was the driving force for Britain's economic growth and industrial development – supporting the building of everything from roads and bridges to canals and beautiful, large buildings. It is impossible to understand how Britain became a world power and modernised without understanding the contribution that slavery made to financing it.

Slavery gave us the City of London

The transatlantic slave trade was also instrumental in the development of Britain's financial institutions, making it the global financial centre that it is today.

We have to remember that while slavery was a hugely profitable venture, it needed a lot of capital upfront to build ships and pay workers, much of which was often lost, as seafarers died or ships capsized in treacherous storms. Therefore, banks played a crucial role in financing voyages and plantations, providing the necessary upfront capital for merchants and investors. Prominent banks still operating and profiting today, such as Barclays and the Royal

Bank of Scotland, have historical ties to the slave trade, with their founders and early investors hugely benefiting from the commerce in human lives.[2]

Insurance companies also thrived by underwriting slave ships and cargoes. The risks associated with the long voyages necessitated insurance, creating a lucrative market for companies willing to cover these ventures. Lloyd's of London, one of the world's leading insurance brokers, has roots in insuring slave ships and their human cargo.

The wealth generated from the slave trade and plantation economies also found its way into the burgeoning stock exchanges of Britain. Investors sought opportunities to increase their wealth, and the profits from the slave trade provided the capital for investments in various sectors. The London Stock Exchange, established in 1801, benefited from the influx of capital derived from the slave economy. Investments in infrastructure, such as railways and ports, were partly funded by the wealth accumulated through the exploitation of enslaved people.

Slavery gave us our clothes

But it wasn't just the massive profits derived from slave labour that made the Britain we know today. Cotton, cultivated in the American South, became a cornerstone of Britain's Industrial Revolution. The raw cotton produced from slave labour was essential for British textile mills.

Britain's cotton industry was a major driver of economic growth, leading to advancements in technology and the establishment of factories, employing thousands of UK workers, both men and women.

In turn, the demand for cotton textiles made in the UK and then sold abroad led to a huge expansion of the British economy, making it a global industrial power. Without the export of cotton, we wouldn't have had the chains that Lenny talked about in Chapter 2, for example.

The rise of the textile industry also had a ripple effect on other sectors in the UK. The need for more efficiency and machinery led to innovations in engineering and manufacturing. It could even be argued that while the transatlantic slave trade was not directly responsible for the steam engine, it certainly fuelled its development, revolutionising transportation and other industries, further propelling economic growth.

Slavery gave us Britain's modern cities

The transatlantic slave trade spurred the growth of British ports and the maritime industry. Prior to slavery, London had been the centre of economic activity in the UK. But with slavery, and its related industries such as textiles, ports such as Liverpool, Sheffield and Bristol became hubs of commerce. Shipbuilding flourished, as a steady supply of vessels was needed to transport goods and enslaved people across the Atlantic. Canals were built in the UK to transport goods back and forth from the new centres of activity. The prosperity of these port cities was directly linked to their involvement in the slave trade, creating jobs and fostering economic development.

The goods produced by enslaved labour, such as sugar, tobacco and cotton, became staples of British trade. The importation of these commodities stimulated domestic industries, such as sugar refining and textile manufacturing. The export of manufactured goods to Africa and the Americas created a cycle of commerce that was highly profitable for British merchants and manufacturers.

The wealth generated from this trade cycle had far-reaching effects on the British economy. It funded those public works, such as roads and canals, which itself facilitated further economic growth. It also contributed to the rise of a wealthy merchant class, whose investments spurred innovation and industrialisation.

Slavery gave us many of Britain's universities and museums

The profits from the transatlantic slave trade allowed for significant wealth accumulation among British merchants, plantation owners and investors. This wealth facilitated social mobility, enabling individuals and families to rise in social status and influence. The newly wealthy often invested in land, real estate and other ventures, further embedding the economic benefits of the slave trade into the fabric of British society. How we understand class and the creation of the middle class was radically influenced by slavery.

This, in turn, had huge cultural implications. Philanthropy became a common way for wealthy individuals to gain social prestige. Many of Britain's educational (Eton), cultural (the National Gallery) and religious institutions (Church of England) benefited from donations and endowments from individuals who had profited from the slave trade. Universities (Cambridge University), museums (the British Museum), and charitable organisations (the King's Fund) were often funded by this wealth, leaving a lasting legacy.

Slavery gave us the United Kingdom

Finally, there is a strong argument that we wouldn't even have a United Kingdom if it hadn't been for the transatlantic slave trade.

The 1707 Act of Union between England and Scotland – creating the United Kingdom of Great Britain, a precursor to the United Kingdom we have today – was negotiated at a very challenging time for Scotland. Scotland had lost a quarter of its liquid capital in a failed trading venture in Panama, and it therefore needed money.

Crucially, Article 4 of the Union Act 1707 gave Scots the right to trade in any British port. This enabled Scottish people to benefit from the spoils of the transatlantic slave system and allowed them to get back on their feet – the trading elite, at least.

So what did slavery do for us, you ask? It literally gave us the Britain we know today.

◆

Lenny: Thank you, Marcus. Teachers all over the country should just read that at the beginning of Black History Month and give the pupils the rest of the month off to think about it! Wow. What a testimony.

Now I know Marcus loves a polemic, and is a fan of the hyperbole, but while some historians might dispute the extent that the transatlantic slave trade is solely responsible for all these

WHAT DID SLAVERY EVER DO FOR US?   61

things, there is little dispute that the slave trade was a cornerstone of Britain's economic development during the sixteenth to nineteenth centuries. The wealth generated from the exploitation of enslaved Africans was at the centre of the growth of Britain's industry, finance and trade, transforming Britain into a global economic power. If Black slaves were *Life of Brian*'s plotters against the Brits, certainly they'd be the butt of one of the unfunniest jokes in history.

The next question, however, is: if this is the debt that Britain owes to slavery, what does the country now owe to the descendants of the enslaved? The fact is, this immense prosperity came at an enormous human cost, with millions of Africans subjected to unimaginable suffering and dehumanisation.

To answer that question, Marcus and I decided – just like they do in *Who Wants to Be a Millionaire?* – to call in a friend . . .

6: DOING THE MATHS

'Hello, hello, hello?'
　'Hello, Lenny. Hi, Marcus!!'
　'Hi, Robert . . . Hang on . . . I can't hear you?'
　'What's that you're saying?'
　'There you are.'
　'At last – hello!'
　'Great to see you, finally.'
　'For cryin' out l— You're still on mute.'
　'HELLO???'
OK, it wasn't the most auspicious start to a Zoom call, but it would – by the time it ended – give Marcus and me a whole new perspective on reparations.

The truth is – despite knowing that the modern global economy was literally built on the labour of enslaved Africans; despite knowing that the British government borrowed a massive 40 per cent of the national budget to compensate former slave owners, the largest such compensation in history; and despite knowing that any reparations package would require not just financial compensation to the descendants of the victims of the transatlantic slave trade but a whole restructuring of our education system and other parts of British society – Marcus and I were still thinking in terms of millions of pounds in compensation to the Black descendants of former enslaved Africans.

A couple of billion pounds at most.

We were wrong – which is why it was so good to go to an expert.

DOING THE MATHS

Robert Beckford is the kind of guy you definitely want as your 'Phone a friend' if you're ever on *Who Wants to Be a Millionaire?* And it wouldn't surprise me if he was banned from doing every pub quiz in the UK.

His big brain came across when I asked him the simplest of questions at the beginning of the Zoom call: 'Great to see you Robert, it's been a long time, where are you at now?'

His answer also proved why it's so hard to pin him down for a chat. 'Well, Lenny, I'm a union of three places. I'm at the University of Winchester, where I'm the professor of Climate and Social Justice, which is really just developing projects that help the public to understand the interface between climate and racial justice.

'I then have another role with a seminary because my main discipline is theology. So I still teach theology at Queen's College, Birmingham, supervising Black students who are taking PhDs. Because there's a real shortage, you know, of Black people with PhDs in the humanities in theology. And then I also work with Vrije University in Amsterdam. And that's great because they're really old-school liberal.'

Nobody can pin this guy down: he's like the Black Pimpernel!

By the way, we never discovered whether he was doing the Zoom in Amsterdam, Winchester or Birmingham and I was too scared to ask just in case he wasn't in any of those places and would start telling us about a fourth project he was doing.

The main reason we were calling was because we knew he would be the best person to talk to about calculating how much Britain should pay in reparations. This is because he – in addition to all the work he is doing currently – has also been making films about slavery and reparations issues for over twenty years.

For instance, in 1999 he worked on the Channel 4 series *Britain's Slave Trade*. In 2005 he presented the Channel 4 documentary *The Empire Pays Back*, and in 2021 he made the film *After the Flood: The Church, Slavery and Reconciliation*. This is just a sample of his output – the list of his academic work and written journalism on slavery and reparations is far too long to even attempt to summarise here.

Beckford is a firm believer in the idea of reparations and, as a theologian, he believes you can trace its origins, and the moral framework, back to the teachings in the Torah and Bible – both Old and New Testament.

Throughout the Old Testament, repentance is usually in the form of making sacrifices.

But, for Beckford, it was at the tender age of ten, when learning the New Testament story of Zacchaeus, that the penny dropped and he began his journey in understanding, and finally campaigning, for reparations.

Now for those of you that didn't go to Sunday school, or like me fell asleep halfway through colouring in the picture of a white Jesus, let me briefly explain the story of Zacchaeus: he was a tax collector who took money from the poor. Long story short, Jesus visits Zacchaeus' house despite him being an evil tax collector and according to Luke 19:8–9:

> Zacchaeus stood up and said to the Lord, 'Look, Lord! Here and now I give half of my possessions to the poor, and if I have cheated anybody out of anything, I will pay back four times the amount.'
>
> Jesus said to him, 'Today salvation has come to this house.'

In Beckford's mind, Britain has certainly committed a crime against the Africans it enslaved, but unlike Zacchaeus it has yet to pay back what it 'cheated' them/us out of. And to pay back is the only route for anyone, or any country, to achieve salvation.

OK, so that was the theological lesson for the day – which I had not expected – but Marcus and I were on our own mission. The reason for the Zoom call was that we wanted to know *how much* Britain should pay back and how to work it out.

But before revealing the number and explaining the working out – in addition to reminding us of the Bible's classic teachings – Beckford had a few words of caution:

Like Esther Stanford-Xosei, in Chapter 3, he wanted to make sure that Marcus and I didn't just think reparations were about money alone.

'Reparations concern every aspect of repairing the damage done to us by transatlantic chattel slavery – economic, social, cultural and spiritual repair. So we look at the damage in each of those categories and explore how we repair it. For example, we might look at cultural damage.'

He went on to explain that in some Caribbean countries the 'cultural repair' might mean developing better links with African countries by creating cultural programmes.

'Social repair' could look at the fact that for the last 400 years African lives have been undervalued by society and this has been absorbed by the descendants of the enslaved. So we need to look at how Black people build self-respect and self-esteem.

When it comes to 'spiritual repair', Beckford explained that it might be looking at African religious practices before slavery took place, as well as examining our religious practices today.

While this had echoes of Esther's definition of reparations, Beckford was also clear that in any discussion around reparations, money must be central to it. Or as Beckford put it, 'economic repair'.

You cannot have reparations without putting a monetary value on it.

So how do you calculate how much Britain owes in reparations exactly?

Beckford went on to explain that there is an established British and international legal framework for compensation – specifically for war crimes – and this can help with the calculations.

The transatlantic slave trade was first acknowledged internationally as a war crime by the UN during the World Conference against Racism, Racial Discrimination, Xenophobia and Related Intolerance, held in Durban, South Africa, in the summer of 2001.

According to Beckford, once you accept that slavery is a war crime, the calculations are relatively straightforward: 'In Britain, we have three levers to calculate compensation – they are loss of earnings; unjust enrichment; and pain and suffering. And you can measure these three things for any kind of crime or wrongdoing – from losing an arm in a car crash to a family friend being murdered.'

(The compensation for losing an arm in a car crash in the UK is set at approximately £21,000 – I think my arms are worth a whole heap more than that, but that is another story.)

Taking the first, 'loss of earnings', calculating reparations involves historical valuation, which attempts to estimate the economic value of the labour extracted from enslaved people. This method considers the wages that would have been paid to enslaved people if they had been free labourers. And this in itself involves three specific numbers:

1. **An estimate of unpaid wages**
    To estimate unpaid wages, historians and economists look at the average wages for similar labour during the period of slavery. For example, if the average wage for agricultural labour

DOING THE MATHS

in the eighteenth century was £20 per year, and an enslaved person worked for twenty years, the unpaid wages would be £400 per person. However, it could be argued that enslaved Africans did receive some compensation for their labour, in the form of food, clothes and shelter. (This part of the calculation annoys me and I'm trying very hard not to let my emotions come into the maths – but damn, my ancestors are wearing sackcloth overalls and shoes made out of tyres and you're saying that's compensation??? HELL NO!)

2. **Adjustments for price changes over time**

    The historical wages minus the payment in kind need to be adjusted for price changes over time – more simply known as inflation – to reflect their value in today's currency. This involves using historical inflation rates to convert past wages into present-day values.

And finally you multiply this by:

3. **Estimates of the number of enslaved people**

    Accurate records of the number of enslaved people transported and sold by British traders are necessary to estimate the total unpaid wages. These records include ship logs, sales records and plantation records.

That is just the start.

Next you need to look at 'unjust enrichment'. This category basically covers everything we listed in the last chapter. But it is not only how the transatlantic slave trade contributed to Britain's economy, it also covers the idea of 'intergenerational wealth transfers'.

The 'unjust enrichment' factor can be broken down into three broad categories:

1. **Contribution to British wealth**
   Estimating the contribution of slavery to British wealth involves analysing the profits generated from slave-produced goods such as sugar, cotton and tobacco. These goods were significant to the British economy and contributed to the wealth of British merchants, investors and the economy as a whole.

2. **Impact on colonial economies**
   The economic impact on colonial economies includes the exploitation of natural resources and the development of infrastructure using enslaved labour. This analysis considers the long-term economic benefits derived from slavery.

3. **Intergenerational wealth transfers**
   The wealth generated from slavery was often invested in other economic ventures, including banking, industry and real estate. This wealth transfer across generations has contributed to economic disparities that persist to this day.

And finally, we have to calculate 'pain and suffering' – which, aside from premature death itself, you can classify into these three broad groups:

1. **Physical abuse**
   This covers everything from beatings, whippings and other forms of corporal punishment that were commonly used to enforce compliance and discipline, to the use of devices such as iron muzzles, collars and shackles, which were employed to punish and control enslaved individuals.

2. **Poor living conditions**
   Slaves lived in overcrowded and unsanitary conditions, often in small, dilapidated huts. Lack of proper shelter exposed them

DOING THE MATHS

to harsh weather, leading to illnesses and physical discomfort. This was frequently combined with inadequate or poor nutrition, which also increased the likelihood and prevalence of disease.

3. Lack of medical care
Access to medical care was minimal or non-existent; injuries and illnesses were often untreated. Common ailments included infections, respiratory diseases and untreated wounds.

These are all very broad categories, and Marcus and I know that there is even more that we could have covered here. If you really want to break down each category we suggest you buy a copy of *Britain's Black Debt: Reparations for Caribbean Slavery and Native Genocide* by Hilary Beckles. But I think this is enough to explain the point Beckford was making.

Now, when Robert Beckford made the programme *The Empire Pays Back* he brought together a group of three experts to, for the first time ever, publicly calculate how much Britain owes in reparations.

The programme was made for television, and so might not have been the most rigorous attempt at explaining very technical and extensive academic research, but the numbers for the three categories Beckford had explained to us roughly broke down as follows:

First, 'loss of earnings' equated to a staggering £4 trillion – in other words, that's £200 per slave, adjusted for inflation brings that to £1 million, multiplied by 4 million slaves . . .

Second, Robert and his team calculated 'unjust enrichment' to be £2.5 trillion. They believed the British economy benefited to the tune of £5 million a year annually for approximately a hundred years. Again, adjusting this for inflation you get to £2.5 trillion.

Third and last, but not least, the calculation for 'pain and suffering' came in at £1 trillion. They calculated that each enslaved African endured £250,000 worth of harm in today's money – and simply multiplied that by the 4 million of enslaved people.

That meant that Britain – having directly enslaved 4 million people – owed £7.5 trillion to the descendants of enslaved Africans!

However, Robert Beckford and his team did this calculation in 2005 and he now thinks that he might have got it wrong. And it is all down to whether you use the British or American framework to calculate reparations.

'The Americans add on loss of labour, which is another way of saying 'freedom'. And they also separate out sexual violence from pain and suffering as well. So they end up with five categories. You can then measure all of those five using international compensation metrics.'

Luckily for us, just a few months previously, an internationally renowned group of specialists on reparations, including Robert Beckford as a consultant, did just this calculation.

In Beckford's own words this was 'the most sophisticated report ever, on detailing how much is owed'.

This 115-page report – known colloquially as the Brattle Report – was introduced by His Excellency Judge Patrick Robinson, and written by Coleman D. Bazelon, Alberto Vargas, Rohan Janakiraman and Mary M. Olson.[1]

Judge Robinson is a Jamaican who was a judge of the International Court of Justice from February 2015 to 2024; prior to this he was the president of the International Criminal Tribunal for the Former Yugoslavia and so he knows a thing or two about international war crimes and justice.

DOING THE MATHS

The Brattle Report didn't just look at Britain but all the 'Western' countries that benefited from the transatlantic slave trade. It calculated all the money owed to the Caribbean and Americas. According to the report:

> Each enslaved person experienced overwhelming harm, beginning with the loss of their liberty and often ending with a premature death after a life marked by personal injury and other forms of violence, if they survived the Middle Passage. By our estimates, these harms were inflicted on 19 million people over the span of four centuries. These 19 million include those Africans kidnapped and transported to the Americas and Caribbean and those born into slavery.

Using the broad criteria Beckford outlined, they calculated that the total harm caused to enslaved Africans due to the transatlantic slave trade, and their descendants, came to a staggering £101 trillion! For context, that is larger than the collective economic activity of all the countries in the world combined (GDP), which in 2021 was £96 trillion!!

I'll be honest, I am not usually one for exclamation marks – but I think they are appropriate here.

According to the report, Portugal today owes £16 trillion (sixty-three times its annual GDP), while America owes almost £21 trillion (slightly less than its GDP in 2021).

And the Brattle Report calculation for how much Britain owes specifically, was significantly larger than Beckford's original calculation. The Brattle Report calculated that Britain owes not £7.5 trillion but almost three times that amount – £18.6 trillion in reparations.

Now the report did not detail how much is owed to Black Britons, but it did detail how much is owed to each country. For instance, Marcus and I are both originally from Jamaica – and the report calculated that the UK should pay £7.4 trillion to Jamaica in reparations.

The Brattle Report blew my mind.

£18.62 trillion.

That's it. Mind blown. POW!!!!!

When we started researching this issue, I honestly thought we might be talking about a couple of million pounds, maybe a billion.

So far Marcus and I agreed with everything Robert Beckford had argued but then he said something I am still questioning: 'All I'm asking is for us all to do the maths. Tell us what you actually did. Because unless that happens, people will not completely understand the terror that was done to Black people.'

Doing the maths is important but we wanted to go further.

The questions Marcus and I were now asking were: who should pay? And how should Black people receive our money?

Maths is good – money is better.

(I would like it in pound coins, please, so I can swim in it like Scrooge McDuck.)

£18.62 trillion. Wow. Or, as Amazon boss Jeff Bezos probably calls it, *runnin'-around money* . . .

6.5: SINS OF OUR FATHERS (AND MOTHERS)

Whilst planning this book together, Marcus would often come to my house on a weekend and we would have 'Saturday soup'. For those who don't know, Saturday soup – Jamaicans pronounce it: 'Sat-deh soup' – is the tradition of preparing soup every Saturday that is common throughout Jamaican households and is essentially a means of using up every single last vegetable in the cupboard and the last piece o' mutton before the big-food-style Sunday dinner the next day. Over the years it has helped households stretch their food from here to back a yard.

Even if I say so myself, I cook a mean Saturday soup (usually with red peas, mutton and dumplin'). Now, if you're not Jamaican and your mother did not pass down her recipe to you then I would highly recommend Melissa Thompson's recipe for 'red pea soup' in her book *Motherland*. (I also love *Rustie Lee's Caribbean Cookbook*, but I digress . . .)

Marcus would come round for Saturday soup and we'd discuss what we were going to write in the next few chapters, and how the book was going generally.

It was at this point, as we prepared to write Chapter 7, that I realised something was slightly wrong. I felt there was a blouse-and-skirt elephant in the room that needed to be addressed before we could answer the questions at the end of Chapter 6.

To use a biblical reference, that metaphorical elephant was, 'Are we responsible for the sins of our fathers?'

Specifically, should white people currently living in Britain, who've never owned slaves, or put a single African on a slave ship – white folks who object to the idea of slavery just as much as I do – be made to pay for the crimes of ancestors they've never met or even know much about? (This line of thinking led to the playtext at the back of the book . . .)

Another question: should Black people living today really be paid compensation for crimes that were committed over a century ago against ancestors *they* probably don't know much about?

Marcus and I do not record our Saturday soup sessions, so what you're about to read is not an exact transcript of a conversation we had on one of those days, but I think it accurately captures the issues I felt we had to grapple with before we could move on to the next chapter.

The Livin' Saturday Soup Conversation

Lenny: Marcus, the question is whether current generations are responsible for the crimes of previous generations. Now, I am not a particularly religious person (although Mama forced me to go to Sunday school with Brother Shepherd in a van with no suspension), but the Bible does use the term 'sins of our fathers' and I was definitely taught that 'the children of those who sin do in fact inherit the seed of sin . . .' I'm not sure I can base the whole argument for reparations on a few lines from the Bible. So how do you think we make this argument, because I definitely don't feel responsible for the sins of my father? (Not even the one where he hit me for hitting my sister Sharon with a stick and it wasn't even that big a hit, but Sharon just was actin' extra and I got beat cos she

SINS OF OUR FATHERS (AND MOTHERS)

was showin' off, cryin' cos there was an *adult* in the room – sorry, I digress again.)

Marcus: This is a massive moral and philosophical question. The fundamental issue – as we've already laid out in the book so far – is that while the individuals directly involved in slavery are no longer alive, the repercussions of slavery continue, with some people still directly – and indirectly – benefiting from those repercussions, while others are still feeling the negative effects.

Lenny: Cutting out all the polite talk, what you are really saying, Marcus, is white people in Britain today are still benefiting from slavery that took place over a century ago, while Black people are still feeling the unfortunate consequences.

Marcus: OK, excuse the pun but yes, you've made the point a lot more Black and white. That is what I am saying. The argument is that societies exist as continuous entities over time – they don't just stop or have walls in between that mean you can totally ignore certain parts and move on. The continuity implies that current members inherit both the benefits and responsibilities of their predecessors, and by extension, they also create future impacts for their successors, like what's happening with climate change. That means that moral responsibility involves acknowledging and addressing historical injustices that persist through generations and, ideally, aiming to correct them as soon as feasibly possible.

Lenny: Therefore, whites in this society, whose predecessors were slave owners, or whites who benefited from the slave trade, even if those predecessors thought they were not being 'bad' by being slavers, should now pay reparations?

Marcus: Precisely – the argument would be that as slavery built the entire British economy, which all Britons benefited from to some extent, then all white British people should pay. And on the other side – if you buy the argument that the idea of race and racism was born out of the transatlantic slave trade (see Chapter 3), then all Black people to this day still suffer the consequences and deserve compensation.

Lenny: I'm not sure I one hundred per cent buy that. We're eating Saturday soup in my very nice kitchen and neither of us are living in poverty, while a few miles away I know that there are white people who are really struggling to make ends meet and even using food banks. How can they be the beneficiaries of slavery, and people like us the victims – leading to the result that they are meant to give you and me money?

Marcus: By that argument you'd ask why should poor people pay taxes that pay for schools, roads and other services that rich people benefit from. The rich people should pay more in tax – agreed – but most people generally agree that in a just society, everyone should pay some amount of tax.

Lenny: That's not the right argument. Poor people also use the schools and roads or, at least in principle, should be given the opportunity to. In reparations you will have poor white people seeing some of their tax money going to Black British folk with more money than them. All for a crime that happened before they or their great-grandparents or even great-great-great-grandparents were even born.

Marcus, I honestly think this is the weakest part of our argument. You are the weakest link, goodbye!

SINS OF OUR FATHERS (AND MOTHERS)

Marcus: I hear you. But let me explain more clearly.

First of all, I think we both agree that racism leads to a worse society for everyone. So solving racism is in everyone's interests – poor or rich, white or Black – and if we think reparations are key to solving racism, then there is no doubt poor white people will benefit from this metaphorical road that they are paying for.

Second, we should break down who are the ongoing beneficiaries of the transatlantic slave trade. I would break it down into three groups: countries, organisations and individuals. The latter could include people like members of the Trevelyan family, which directly owned more than 1,000 enslaved Africans over six plantations in Grenada, who have gone on record to say they want to pay reparations (more on that in Chapter 7).

Lenny: Right . . . so it's not about whether some random poor guy on the poverty line should give you their hard-earned cash?

Marcus: Precisely. The question is whether the current British government is responsible for crimes committed by successive British governments years ago. Is the current board of Lloyd's of London responsible for crimes committed by the company over a century ago? And are descendants of individuals who owned and benefited from the unpaid labour of slaves now responsible for the 'sins of their fathers'?

By the way – your Saturday soup is fire today! Do you have a Supermalt to go with this?

Lenny: I feel like we're getting somewhere now. I think I can answer this one. It makes sense that a country must be responsible for the actions done in its name in the past, otherwise every new government could just wipe out any debt that the previous government borrowed. Countries by definition must be larger, and their responsibilities last longer, than any single generation.

And, no. You know I don't have any Supermalt – you ask that every time you come over. I've got carrot juice or council pop. Choose.

Marcus: And the same goes for companies. They have to take the rough with the smooth. If the people who run companies and their employees are reaping the benefits of the company being in business for the last 200-plus years, then they must also be responsible for the debts of that company, be that a financial loan the company took out 200 years ago, or a moral loan. Carrot juice, please – you're a gent.

Lenny: In many ways, companies and countries are the easy ones, because they were literally alive at the time the crimes were committed. If you think about it, it's not a matter of them being responsible for the 'sins of their fathers'. If a company or country lasts longer than the life of an individual, then they are responsible for their own actions. I hope I am making sense here?

Marcus: I'm still following.

Lenny: Surprisingly – and I hadn't thought about this until we started talking – the responsibility of the individuals is the harder one. Even if their great-great-great-grandparents owned enslaved Africans, the individuals alive today did not participate in the historical injustices and so should they really be held accountable for actions they did not take themselves? Holding current generations responsible seems unjust.

They really bear no *direct* culpability for past crimes.

Marcus: For me it is the exact opposite – asking the rich individuals who have direct links to their forefathers and foremothers owning slaves to pay reparations is the easiest one of the three.

It isn't about whether they are responsible for the original crime. It is whether they are still benefiting from the proceeds of that crime. So it is less about punishing them for the 'sins of their fathers', it is about them returning the proceeds of the crime of which they are in possession.

Lenny: So you are saying, if my grandad stole a painting and gave it to me, I should give the painting back to the rightful owner – even though I didn't steal it?

Marcus: Yes!

Lenny: I never knew my grandfather, but if he's the one who gave us that painting of Jesus at the Last Supper paying the tab – big respect, but he can absolutely have it back . . .

OK, you've convinced me. Let's move on to the next chapter, then, and answer the questions posed at the end of Chapter 6: who should pay reparations and how should Black people receive our money? Also – when can that happen?

Marcus: Not so fast. Before we started this Saturday soup session I didn't need much convincing that present generations should pay for the crimes committed by their ancestors. But now I am unsure whether Black people today – you and me – should be compensated for crimes that were not directly inflicted on us.

Lenny: Wow, Marcus! Sometimes I think you overthink

things. Let's try and wrap this up quickly because we've eaten all the soup and you'll miss the last train home if you're not careful.

I've looked into this and there are basically two arguments as to why we should be compensated for crimes committed against generations before we even existed. The first I'll call the 'bad apartment' argument, and the second I'll call the 'cash in the attic' argument.

Marcus: So, what is the 'bad apartment' argument?

Lenny: I got this one from an academic called Janna Thompson who is based in Australia. She said that suppose builders construct a terrible apartment tower ignoring all the safety regulations and breaking the law. And then suppose the building falls down fifty years later killing and injuring everyone in it. The people entitled to compensation are not just the people who moved in when the building was first built but all the people that were born and lived in the building long after.

If we believe the effects of slavery are still causing us harm, then right now multiple metaphorical buildings are falling down every day and causing us injury. It doesn't matter that the original crime of slavery happened way before we were born.

Marcus: That echoes Kehinde Andrews' Malcolm X quote way back in Chapter 3: 'If you stick a knife in my back nine inches and pull it out six inches, there's no progress. If you pull it all the way out, that's not progress. The progress is healing the wound that's below, that the blow made.' Sticking in the knife is the act of enslaving Africans in the first place. Pulling it out six inches is ending slavery, but we still need the wound to heal. That is giving us – Black people living today – reparations.

OK – I buy the 'bad apartment' argument, what's the 'cash in the attic' argument?

Lenny: That's really straightforward. It is about us receiving the inheritance that is owed to us. Inheritance is passed down from generation to generation. If someone steals my grandmother's money so I can't inherit it, that's unfair, and I have a right to that inheritance.

Enslaved Africans were denied both the wages they should have earned and the compensation for the way they were treated. If they had been given this they would have been able to pass it down to their sons and daughters, who would have been able to pass it down to their sons and daughters, etc. Just as the descendants of slave owners were able to receive the wealth from slavery.

If we believe in the principle of inheritance, then there is 'cash in the attic' that should be given to us. I'd like mine now, please.

Marcus: Len, that soup was boombastic, you know – you got any I can take home?

Lenny: Yeah. That'll be £15, please, for the large Tupperware of soup with hard food and some mutton.

Marcus: Bit steep. But it was the bomb. Can you lend me £15?

Lenny: Sure. Just lemme go and sell my grandad's painting . . .

◆

And that, people, is how a Marcus and Lenny Saturday soup session works.

And here is my recipe.

Lenny's Saturday Soup

Ingredients

- 2 lb beef or chicken (with bones)
- 1 onion, chopped
- 2 cloves garlic, minced
- 2 carrots, sliced
- 2 stalks scallion, chopped
- 1 piece thyme
- 2 potatoes, diced
- 1 yam, diced
- 1 chocho (chayote), diced
- ½ lb pumpkin, diced
- 1 Scotch bonnet pepper (whole)
- 4 cups water/chicken stock
- Salt and pepper to taste
- Dumplings (optional):
  - 1 cup flour
  - Pinch of salt
  - Water (enough to form dough)

Instructions

1. Prepare meat:
   - Clean and cut the meat into pieces.
   - In a large pot, brown the meat with onion and garlic.
2. Simmer:
   - Add water or chicken stock to the pot.
   - Bring to a boil, then reduce heat and let simmer for about 45 minutes, skimming off any foam.
3. Add vegetables:
   - Add carrots, potatoes, yam, chocho, pumpkin, scallion, thyme and Scotch bonnet pepper to the pot.
   - Season with salt and pepper.
4. Soup mix (optional):
   - Stir in the Grace Cock Soup Mix for added flavour.

SINS OF OUR FATHERS (AND MOTHERS)

5. Make dumplings (optional):
   - Mix flour and salt in a bowl.
   - Gradually add water, kneading until a smooth dough forms.
   - Roll into small balls or cylinders and add to the pot.
6. Cook:
   - Simmer for another 30–45 minutes until vegetables and dumplings are tender.
   - Adjust seasoning to taste.
7. Serve:
   - Remove the Scotch bonnet pepper before serving.
   - Serve hot and enjoy!

Lenny's top tips

- Spice level: be cautious with the Scotch bonnet; it's very spicy. Keep it whole for flavour without heat, or pierce for more spice.
- Variations: you can add corn, green bananas, or your choice of ground provisions.
- Protein: swap beef or chicken for pork or add salted meats for additional flavour.

Enjoy your hearty and delicious Jamaican Saturday soup!

◆

If you've enjoyed this little philosophical detour, then I'd definitely recommend *Should Current Generations Make Reparation for Slavery?* by Janna Thompson. It goes into these arguments in more detail. A small book that carries a big punch.

Now let's get to Chapter 7.

7: REPARATIONS VERSUS CHARITY

In 1985, I helped launch a small charity in response to the famine in Ethiopia. The idea behind it was simple: could we harness the power of laughter to raise money and help people in need?

We had our first fundraising event in April 1986. It was a three-day fundraising show staged at the Shaftesbury Theatre in London with comedians like Rowan Atkinson, Billy Connolly and Stephen Fry. We were even able to rope in a pop star or two, including Kate Bush and Cliff Richard.

Two years later, after I had visited Ethiopia to see the results of the work we were trying to do, the show moved to TV and we hosted our first night of comedy on the BBC. That first fundraiser generated £15 million and attracted 30 million viewers. The charity now raises money for numerous organisations helping children in need and tackling worldwide poverty with a particular focus on Africa.

If you haven't figured it out by now, I am talking about Comic Relief and it's one of my proudest achievements. It is fair to say that we have made mistakes along the way but for nearly forty years there is no doubt in my mind that it has been a force for good. It has raised over a billion pounds so far and I expect it will raise much more.

In 2024, I hosted my last Red Nose Day, Comic Relief's annual fundraising telethon, and after I left the television studio I went home almost in tears. The emotion just overcame me – everything the charity had achieved over the years, the natural adrenaline comedown after performing live, and the grief of saying goodbye to something that has been part of my life since I was in my twenties.

I mention all this because of a question that Marcus asked me at one of our Saturday soup sessions.

'What do you think is the difference between reparations and charity, if any?'

I believe in reparations. Uncontroversially, I believe that slavery is a moral wrong, and for all the reasons we have outlined in the previous chapters, it's evident that the descendants of enslaved Africans are owed a massive, massive debt.

I also believe in charity: that people who find themselves in more fortunate positions have a duty to help those people who are worse off than themselves.

The reality is that, when it comes to charity, the reason some people find themselves in more fortunate positions than others is due to history. And here is where Marcus's question comes in, about the blurred line between reparations and charity.

Leaving aside the sums we're talking about, the question is if white people – in general – are in a more fortunate position than Black people – in general – due to the history of transatlantic slavery; how is giving money to the descendants of enslaved Africans, and calling that 'reparations', any different from the great British public giving money to poor Black people and calling it 'charity'?

Officially, conventional wisdom states that reparations are a demand for justice, an acknowledgement of responsibility, and a way to make things right for a victim or community. As we've already explained, reparations can include restitution, compensation, rehabilitation, guarantees of non-repetition and public apologies.

But if we focus on the money part of reparations, isn't that just the same as charity?

Indeed, in recent years we have seen numerous organisations and individuals with direct links to slavery make 'reparations'. Or even if they haven't directly used the word 'reparations' themselves, others have commonly understood their donations to be 'reparations'.

For example, Lloyd's of London, who made substantial profits by insuring slave ships, issued this statement in 2020: 'Lloyd's has a long and rich history dating back over 330 years, but there are some aspects of our history that we are not proud of . . . In particular, we are sorry for the role played by the Lloyd's market in the eighteenth and nineteenth century slave trade. This was an appalling and shameful period of English history, as well as our own, and we condemn the indefensible wrongdoing that occurred.' The insurer then went on to announce it would be investing £40 million to help impacted communities.[1]

The brewer Greene King, through its CEO Nick Mackenzie, also put out a statement in the same year that they would make a 'substantial investment' to benefit the Black and minority ethnic community, and support race diversity in its business, adding: 'It is inexcusable that one of our founders profited from slavery and argued against its abolition in the 1800s.'[2]

Two years prior, in 2018, Glasgow University discovered it had directly benefited financially from the transatlantic slave trade and a year later took the decision to pay £20 million in reparations to the University of the West Indies to fund a centre for development research.

The *Guardian* newspaper, with no direct links to the slave trade, recognised its founders' wealth was built off slavery-related industries and established a wide programme of measures including 'raising awareness of transatlantic slavery and its legacies through partnerships in Manchester and globally; media diversity; further academic research, and increasing the scope and ambition of the Guardian's reporting . . . of Black communities in the UK, US, the Caribbean, South America and Africa'.[3] They also announced, possibly most importantly, £10 million in funds going to the region in Jamaica whose communities were most affected by the newspaper's founders.[4]

This is just the British tip of a far larger iceberg of organisations around the world that have and continue to make payments in response to their direct and indirect roles in the transatlantic slave trade. Interestingly, while some organisations have used the term 'reparations', others, like the Scott Trust which oversees the *Guardian*, have used terms like 'restorative justice' or have just talked about responding to slavery more generally.

But is this just another form of charity, is this really going to be the key to ending racism as Esther Stanford-Xosei said it should be during our *Black British Lives Matter* podcast?

Kehinde Andrews, Britain's first Black Studies professor, has written a great deal on this issue. He is scathing of the way the issue of reparations is currently discussed and presented by most organisations. 'The way that reparations is brought up now, it doesn't really resemble anything that I would think of as reparations.'

Marcus and I didn't ask him about all the different reparation and compensation for slavery schemes that I have just run through, but he did give us one particular example as an explanation.

'Lloyd's of London – who were embedded in the slave trade insuring slave ships, and is today Britain's largest financial entity – following the death of George Floyd, came out and said,

"Actually, we have a problem. We want to pay reparations." But their reparations (or more accurately, response to their involvement in the transatlantic slave trade) is a diversity scheme and a bit of money to charity. I think that's ridiculous. I mean, it's not reparations; that, to me, is just offensive.'

In another interview Kehinde Andrews referred to this sort of practice as 'reparations washing', claiming it was more to do with PR than reparations. 'Giving an apology, making some commitments . . . is not serious.'

Robert Beckford has also been fairly critical of some of the reparations schemes announced by various organisations, and when he spoke to us noted the trend of many organisations 'folding in' their reparations work to their charitable activities. Some are re-labelling what would have previously been seen as charity.

'Right now everybody wants to do "how do we heal?" because they *don't* want to deal with "how much do we owe?",' Beckford told us. '"Maybe we can spend a couple of grand on a new monument or have a big celebration every year and bring everybody together."'

Beckford seems to think most, if not all, of the organisations who are supposedly saying they are paying reparations now are not really asking 'How much do we owe?' Instead they're asking 'How much can we afford?' or, to be really cynical, 'How little can we get away with?'

I'll be honest with you, although Marcus and I both massively respect Robert Beckford, and Kehinde Andrews, we are not sure we agree with their positions.

Or maybe I am less cynical, while Marcus's cynicism is off the scale – so we both end up in the same place.

I find it hard to believe it is all a PR stunt. I honestly believe that organisations are trying to do the right thing. For instance,

REPARATIONS VERSUS CHARITY 89

I know some of the people on the Scott Trust who oversee the *Guardian*'s programme and they seem like very sincere people.

On the other hand, Marcus – who from here on out will be called 'Mr Cynical' – disagrees with Robert Beckford and Kehinde Andrews because he just doesn't believe the organisations *need* the PR. He doesn't believe fewer people will go to pubs owned by Greene King or drink less beer if they don't apologise for their link to slavery, or that fewer people will go to Glasgow University if they don't make reparations.

So, for very different reasons we end up with the same thought: these organisations are genuinely *trying* to make reparations.

While the amount these organisations give in the name of reparations might not be enough, we don't believe there is malicious intent behind what they are doing.

However, it still doesn't answer one of our original questions: how should the money given for reparations be different from charity, if at all?

The answer came from remembering a statue outside BBC Broadcasting House in London.

The statue is of George Orwell.

We all know Orwell's novels, like *1984* and *Animal Farm*, but Marcus is a bit of a George Orwell nut. If you ask him what his favourite writing by George Orwell is, he will tell you it is not a novel, but a short essay simply titled 'Charles Dickens'.

(**Marcus:** My favourite essay by George Orwell is actually 'Shooting an Elephant' but for dramatic licence and for the purpose of this chapter, let's go with 'Charles Dickens'.)

Marcus feels that Orwell's critique of Dickens is directly relevant to answering the question as to the difference between money given in the name of reparations and that given in charity.

To cut a long story short, what Orwell explains is that in his stories, Dickens invariably wants to change the moral character of bad people to act better. A classic example is Ebenezer Scrooge in *A Christmas Carol*. By the end of the book, Scrooge does become a nicer person – treating Bob Cratchit and his family a lot better, for example – but – and here comes Orwell's critique of Dickens' writing – the power dynamic between Scrooge and Cratchit never changes. Ebenezer Scrooge remains the boss, while Bob Cratchit remains the employee.

Scrooge giving the Cratchit family a massive goose for Christmas was an act of charity.

George Orwell's critique of Dickens is that although he tries to make people nicer, morally acceptable, he never actually addresses the fundamental power dynamics that cause the inequality prevalent in so many of his stories.

For me this is the underlying problem of reparations as shaped by so many organisations so far. While they might help the individuals or even the communities, atoning for their participation in the transatlantic slave trade, they never fundamentally address the power dynamic between the two groups. And, until they do, then it is very hard to distinguish this version of reparations from charity.

To use one of the examples we mentioned before, the *Guardian* has a dominant position in global media which it admits was built on the backs of enslaved Africans. But still today, there are no African or Caribbean media organisations that come close to challenging the *Guardian*'s position, and the *Guardian* has so far made no attempt to change this positioning through its reparations work.

Similarly, Lloyd's of London has a dominant position in

global finance that one could also argue is, at least partially, due to its involvement in the transatlantic slave trade. On the other hand, there are no financial organisations, let alone insurance firms, that are run and owned by the descendants of enslaved Africans that even come close to Lloyd's position. And Lloyd's itself has not made any statements that might change the positioning of financial or insurance firms within the industry.

The way Marcus frames it, drawing heavily on George Orwell's critique of Dickens, is that until we have a reparations programme that aims to fundamentally alter the power dynamics between the descendants of the people who profited from slavery and the descendants of the enslaved, you do not really have reparations, you still have a form of charity – irrespective of how much money might have been given.

In many ways this is all about how you view the 'restitution' part of reparations. In law, restitution can be defined as being 'concerned with reversing one party's unfair or unjust benefit at the expense of another party. The purpose of a claim of restitution, therefore, is not to compensate the claimant for a loss but to deprive the defendant of a benefit.'[5]

If one of the benefits that the *Guardian* newspaper or Lloyd's acquired due to slavery is a dominant global position – especially if it is at the cost of organisations owned and run by people of African descent not having the same advantages, then is this not a 'benefit' they should give up?

It is why – even though it can seem like semantics – Marcus believes it is important that the *Guardian* use the term 'restorative justice' and not 'reparations'. The newspaper is doing its best to atone for the sins of its founders but 'reparations' is something different.

It's a compelling argument.

I also think it means that two things can be right at the same time.

Organisations like the *Guardian*, Lloyd's of London and Glasgow University can pay what they genuinely believe they owe, but it can still not be enough. I truly like the idea of organisations trying their best – while at the same time I can see that Kehinde Andrews and Robert Beckford are right in criticising them.

If the act of reparations is about righting historical wrongs and ultimately ending racism, attempts definitely seem to have fallen short of their aims if, after so-called reparations schemes are implemented, all the power *still* resides within the very organisations that got their positions due to the unpaid labour of my ancestors.

Increasingly, the more we researched reparations and asked ourselves the difficult questions, the more it seemed that reparations means so much more than money.

Like the peeling of an onion, the answer to each question seemed to just reveal another layer of difficult questions.

There is no way any organisation that benefited from slavery is going to purposely give up their standing in the world. They may pay back 'what they think they owe', but would that ever be real reparations? Or, to put it differently, and returning to the enormous sums we explained in Chapter 6, if they paid back what some experts have calculated they owe, they'd be bankrupt!

At this point, I felt like simply giving up – but then I came across a newspaper article that gave me something more positive I could hold on to.

In 2023, the BBC correspondent Laura Trevelyan discovered that her family received £26,898 in 1835 in compensation for the end of slavery. That was a huge sum of money back in those

REPARATIONS VERSUS CHARITY

days – indicating that the Trevelyan family must have owned a large number of slaves.

The story of the Trevelyans made the headlines and, in them, Laura pledged £100,000 to the Grenada National Reparations Commission.[6] So far, so normal – and in line with what the organisations we discussed earlier have done. She pledged an amount of money which I am sure was a lot to Laura Trevelyan, but was in no way going to fundamentally change her position in society or her relationship to the Black people around her.

But she also did something extra. She helped create a group of other individuals who had also benefited from the transatlantic slave trade and wanted to give reparations. It was called Heirs of Slavery.

The Heirs of Slavery group was interesting not just because they all donated money for reparations, but because they decided to support what is known as the Ten Point Plan for Reparatory Justice. The plan was created by a group of twenty countries known as the Caribbean Community and Common Market (CARICOM).[7]

Why did the Heirs of Slavery's support for the ten-point plan matter? Well, CARICOM's ten-point plan is actually kind of radical, and Marcus and I both had a feeling that – if implemented – it could take reparations out of charity and change the power dynamic between the descendants of the beneficiaries of the transatlantic slave trade and the descendants of the enslaved.

But we weren't one hundred per cent sure. So once again Marcus and I had to call a friend to help us out.

8: MAKING WAKANDA A REALITY

'I know people have a problem with the *Black Panther* film. But my God, when I went to see it in London, there was a sense of: "This is what it should be like! Yeah! We should be independent! We should have our own infrastructure! Our own source of financial funding! We shouldn't need allies, and we certainly shouldn't need our colonial oppressors to be giving us handouts! We also need turbo-powered, shiny black jet bikes. To hell with minicabs."'

It is really hard not to like Kenneth Mohammed. He's a serious guy but with the kind of warm smile and laugh that make you listen to some really challenging ideas without being defensive.

He is the kind of guy who can reference the made-up country of Wakanda and the most intricate details of the Haitian revolution in the same breath. The kind of guy who can spit lyrics on T'Challa AND bell hooks SIMULTANEOUSLY, bruv, y'get me?

Point is, he really knows his stuff and not just from an academic standpoint but from lived experience.

Raised by a single mother who – in his own words – 'worked her butt off to put me through school in Trinidad', Kenneth Mohammed came to the UK in the 1980s. That's when he first experienced racism. After doing his undergraduate and Master's degrees, he completed a PhD on the legacy of colonialism and how it impacts corruption in the Caribbean.

But possibly most importantly for Marcus and myself, he really understands money. He used to work for Microsoft as Chief Financial Officer in the Eastern and Southern Caribbean region, in charge of twenty-two Caribbean countries. Nevertheless, when he looked at his counterpart in the US, he told us he discovered they were making almost twice his salary.

We needed to talk to Kenneth Mohammed because we were troubled by the idea that companies and individuals were paying off a debt for benefiting from the slave trade while nothing was really changing in the world.

Mohammed has written extensively about reparations in numerous outlets including the *Guardian* and Bloomberg, and sees the concept as so much more than just people 'paying their debt' for what they owe for slavery. He sees it as a way of building a new world, one in which Black talented individuals in the Caribbean are not paid half of what their US counterparts are paid, one in which countries forged out of slavery in the Caribbean and the Americas are on equal footing with the formerly slave-owning countries.

In other words, could reparations create Wakanda – the imaginary country invented by Stan Lee and Jack Kirby in *Black Panther*?

The short answer, according to Mohammed, is an emphatic 'yes'.

But it's not going to be brought about by individuals donating a few grand, or even companies giving millions.

For Mohammed, it is about addressing a deep wrong, a wrong that established the current world order, a wrong that runs so deep that it can only be rectified on an international level – something he sees as a revolutionary act that is born out of the Black struggle for freedom and equality.

'The Caribbean has produced so many activists. We had Marcus Garvey in Jamaica. We also produce people like Frantz Fanon, who I think was from Martinique; Kwame Ture, otherwise known as Stokely Carmichael, originally from Trinidad, who agitated in the Black Power movement. And, of course, you have Bob Marley, who campaigned through his music. For me, this is the background to understanding the modern reparations movement.'

Like the Heirs of Slavery group, he points to the ten-point plan on reparations set out by CARICOM, which we mentioned at the end of the last chapter.

For Mohammed, this plan is the centre of the 'modern reparations movement'.

So here are the basics of plan, in as plain and simple language as we can make it:

1. A full and formal apology for the transatlantic slave trade.
2. An indigenous people's development programme.
3. Funding for voluntary repatriation to Africa.
4. The establishment of cultural institutions and the return of cultural heritage.
5. Assistance in remedying the public health crisis.
6. Education programmes.
7. The enhancement of historical and cultural knowledge exchanges.
8. Psychological rehabilitation as a result of the transmission of trauma.
9. The right to development using technology.
10. Debt cancellation and monetary compensation.

CARICOM's Ten Point Plan was first set out in 2013, but according to Kenneth Mohammed it only really started to gain momentum when Mia Amor Mottley became prime minister of Barbados in 2018.

If you don't know Mia Mottley, she is kind of the Beyoncé of reparations – although did you know Beyoncé actually supports reparations? Maybe they could do a duet together and I could do backing vocals . . .

In 2020 Mottley supercharged the calls for reparations, referring to them as a 'Caribbean Marshall Plan'[1] after the US-funded economic recovery plan for the Western European nations that were devastated in the Second World War. In 2021 she oversaw Barbados becoming a republic – removing the Queen as the head of state and replacing the monarchy with a president – which she framed as the country throwing off its colonial past. And in 2023 she gave a lecture at the London School of Economics demanding a global conversation on reparations for countries that saw their people enslaved, saying, 'The conspiracy of silence has diminished the horror of what our people faced.'[2]

She hasn't quite single-handedly put the CARICOM Ten Point Plan on the map but I doubt it would have got there without her.

Kenneth Mohammed supports the plan but does not consider all ten points to be equal. He led us through what he saw as the most important points and why he saw those as the most effective way to bring about true reparations.

Interestingly, he started off by criticising the first point – the need for a full and formal apology.

'I have a problem with the idea of the apology because I think when you force an apology, is it really genuine? I go back to my childhood in Trinidad, and when I'd bend my brother's arm behind his back and tell him to say sorry, it wasn't a real apology.'

According to the CARICOM Reparations Commission, a

full apology 'accepts responsibility, commits to non-repetition, and pledges to repair the harm caused'.

He points to formal apologies that have already happened but with little effect: 'The Dutch prime minister recently apologised for slavery in Suriname, Aruba, Bonaire and Curaçao, and other former colonies in South America and the Caribbean. Then we had the German president, who expressed shame over what they did in Tanzania and Namibia.'

Instead, Kenneth Mohammed was more in favour of the Caribbean countries looking to international litigation against the former enslaving countries to bring about reparations – one could say the 'legal armlock'. For instance, in 2014, several Caribbean countries attempted to sue the British government for reparations for four centuries of slavery, but Britain used jurisdiction issues arising from the Commonwealth to block the claim.[3]

Mohammed doesn't feel that should be the end of it.

Looking at point two – 'an indigenous people's development programme' – he said understanding the full history and consequences of the transatlantic slave trade is critical. And part of this is recognising that Africans were not the only victims of the transatlantic slave trade.

According to CARICOM, the indigenous populations of the Caribbean were decimated due to slavery. They went from being a community of 3 million people in 1700, to less than 30,000 in 2000. Compensating these communities and recognising their right to land is critical.

Kenneth Mohammed also took us through point four – the establishment of cultural institutions and the return of cultural heritage – which is all about 'the restoration of historical memory through community institutions such as museums and research centres'. I was immediately reminded again of the *Black Panther* movie and the infamous scene where Michael B. Jordan 'liberates' 'stolen' African artefacts from an institution which strongly resembles the British Museum.

Mohammed quickly skipped past points five to seven: assistance in remedying the public health crisis, education programmes and the enhancement of historical and cultural knowledge exchanges. Although he felt these were important, our conversation focused far more on the other remaining points: three, eight, nine and ten.

Point three: funding for voluntary repatriation to Africa.

He opined that understanding and strengthening the links between Africa and the Caribbean is critical to reparations. Personally, I challenge any Black person who has even a modicum of knowledge about Caribbean or American history and does not feel a pull to Africa.

I agree with him that unless we understand the central role Africa plays in Black people's lives, the argument for reparations is almost nonsensical. We are asking for compensation for a crime that originates from us being forcibly removed from our homeland – that homeland is Africa.

Those links can be made both on the personal and the institutional levels. For example, when it comes to institutions, in 2005 the African Union first recognised the African diaspora as crucial to the development of the African continent. This culminated in 2023 when the African Union formally recognised the Caribbean diaspora as the 'sixth African region'. And in 2024 the African Export–Import Bank (Africa's second largest bank) signed a Memorandum of Understanding with the Caribbean Export Development Agency to increase trade and investment between Africa and the Caribbean.[4]

When it comes to the personal connection, in 2019 Ghana launched the 'Year of Return', encouraging the descendants of enslaved Africans to 'return home' – both for tourism as well as for investment. The campaign was timed to commemorate the 400th anniversary of the arrival of the first recorded European ship carrying enslaved Africans to the United States. And in 2021, Sierra Leone became the first African nation to formally give people citizenship if they can prove they have ancestral ties to the country through a simple DNA test.

The links between Africans on the continent and across the diaspora really are everywhere.

Marcus feels really strongly when it comes to point eight: psychological rehabilitation as a result of the transmission of trauma.

These days, when Marcus isn't writing books with me, he's the CEO of the Film and TV Charity, one of whose major missions is to look after the mental health of people working in the screen sector. Although the charity looks after everyone's mental health irrespective of their race, Marcus is the first to tell you that Black people in Britain (the descendants of enslaved Africans) are disproportionately affected by mental ill health. In the UK, rates of psychosis among Black Caribbean people are nine times higher than for white British populations. Many people attribute this directly to our experience of slavery and the unresolved trauma it has caused throughout our communities.

That said, Kenneth Mohammed pointed out that the psychological trauma of slavery manifests itself in numerous different ways and not just in what we think of as mental ill health in the West. For instance, he pointed to the harmful practice of skin bleaching as being just one example of trauma being passed down from generation to generation: 'When I was growing up in the Caribbean, for example, you had to be fair-skinned to be in certain industries, like banking. These mindsets are a direct result of slavery – that being light-skinned, or closer to white, gives you certain social and economic advantages.'

For me, addressing this internalised racism – that I believe affects every Black person to a greater or lesser degree – is critical.

To put it simply – if we see cutting and self-harm as a form of mental illness, then I also believe skin bleaching is a form of self-harm, and our official higher rate of reported mental ill health is just the tip of the iceberg.

The more Kenneth Mohammed explained the CARICOM Ten Point Plan the more it made sense to me, the more it seemed to tackle the root causes of the racism that Black people experience.

As he went through each point, it was obvious that the last two – 'nine: the right to development through the use of technology' and 'ten: debt cancellation and monetary compensation' – were the ones that really excited him.

Explaining the importance of technology transfer in terms of reparations, Mohammed grounded it directly in the history of slavery, using the British slogan that was popular during slavery and colonialism: 'Not a nail is to be made in the colonies.' He explained that this was a deliberate government policy to make sure the Caribbean countries were not able to industrialise and would be dependent on Britain for manufactured goods.

Drawing on his direct experience of working in the oil industry, he said that the policy of withholding technological know-how still impacts to this day. It means that countries with economies formerly based on enslaved Africans – in other words, the Caribbean – are still dependent on the West when it comes to extracting their natural resources, and are unable to compete on the world stage when it comes to manufactured goods.

Time and time again, listening to Kenneth Mohammed, the CARICOM Ten Point Plan just seemed to make sense to me.

This was not reparations in terms of some simple money transfer as I had imagined when Marcus and I first started researching this book.

Nor was it 'well-intentioned but guilty' beneficiaries of historical transatlantic slavery who wanted to pay their debt and help Black people but not ultimately change the power dynamic between the descendants of enslavers and the enslaved (white and Black people).

This was about interrogating all the things that hold Black people back, from racism to underdevelopment, and addressing them one by one on an international level so that the descendants of our forefathers who were brutalised via transatlantic slavery are on an equal footing with the beneficiaries of the transatlantic slave trade.

It really felt like this was a reparations plan that could actually end racism once and for all. Interestingly, money was the very last point in the CARICOM ten-point programme. In the words of Kenneth Mohammed, 'As an accountant, I believe that's the most important thing.'

So let's really explore the last and final point: debt cancellation and monetary compensation.

According to the CARICOM Reparations Commission's website:

> CARICOM governments that emerged from slavery and colonialism have inherited the massive crisis of community poverty and an inability to deal with the development of their countries because of the burdens of the legacy of colonialism . . . This process has resulted in states accumulating unsustainable

levels of public debt that now constitutes 'fiscal entrapment'. Since correcting the burden of colonialism has fallen on these new States, they are unable to deal with the challenges of development without taking on onerous levels of debt. This debt cycle properly belongs to the governments from the responsible European countries who have made no sustained attempt to deal with debilitating colonial legacies. Support for the payment of domestic debt, [and] the cancellation of international debt . . . are necessary reparatory actions to correct the harm caused by colonialism.[5]

In other words, CARICOM governments were saying that the legacy of slavery, and policies such as 'not a single nail to be made in the colonies', left Caribbean countries so poor that they have had to borrow money simply to keep their economies afloat. And that debt is a vicious cycle as the countries have to borrow more money just to pay off their old debt. Cancelling that debt is critical if you are going to properly overcome the legacy of slavery.

I know there will be some people who will say, 'But Len, Marcus, you can't blame everything on slavery when it comes to these countries,' but you can't say it is just a *coincidence* that the countries that became rich due to the transatlantic slave trade are all richer than the countries that were the victims of the transatlantic slave trade. (But if you really want to argue with us, Marcus suggests reading the classic book *Capitalism and Slavery* by Eric Williams – I think he also wrote *The Very Hungry Capitalist*, but I'll have to check.)

Hence, at the very very very end of the CARICOM Reparations Commission's Ten Point Plan – almost an afterthought – the last line in point ten is '. . . and direct monetary payments where appropriate, are necessary reparatory actions to correct the harm caused by colonialism'.

CARICOM might have made it point ten but, like the famous aphorism goes, the last is definitely *not* the least!

Personal direct payments to the descendants of enslaved Africans seems to be low on both CARICOM and Kenneth Mohammed's list of priorities when it came to thinking about reparations. It is payments to the region, as a whole, that are the priority. Making Wakanda in the Caribbean a reality seemed to be far more important to him as he said at the start of our conversation – building countries' and not individuals' wealth.

Marcus and I are big fans of the CARICOM Ten Point Plan. But that doesn't mean we don't have our doubts about it and they broadly fall into three categories: corruption, Black British people, and 'I still want my cheque, DAMN YOU!'

For me the CARICOM plan seems to rely far too much on reparations between countries. If there is one thing that working with Comic Relief has made me wary of, it is relying on governments to deliver the best results for their citizens. We may wish it wasn't so but corruption is a fact of life. While countries like Barbados and the Bahamas fare relatively well according to some world rankings of corruption (24 and 30 respectively on the internationally recognised 'Corruption Perception Index'), other countries like Jamaica and Trinidad and Tobago are lower in the rankings (69 and 76 respectively).[6]

Some would even argue that corruption and bad governance are just another symptom of slavery, which reparations is meant to address, and so the last thing you want to do is put these Caribbean governments in charge of reparations.

However, Mohammed had an answer for that: 'The plan is to set up a CARICOM body to receive any funds in relation to the ten-point programme . . . an independent body which is not political.'

His PhD is on corruption, so I should have some faith in that, but I was also reminded of something Robert Beckford said when I raised the same issue (see Chapter 6). 'When Germany paid 25 billion marks to the Israeli government (in reparations for war crimes against Jewish people), nobody said, "They're just going to fritter it away," or accused them of corruption.' When the British government paid £25 million to slave owners no one thought they didn't deserve it because they wouldn't spend it responsibly.

Mohammed clearly feels there are structural ways to get around the issue of corruption, and implicit in Robert Beckford's answer is that even bringing up the issue belies a degree of internalised racism. I might not think the British government spends my tax money in the best way, but I rarely think of the entire government as corrupt and unworthy of my tax money. Indeed, going back to those corruption indexes, the UK is just one place ahead of the Bahamas.

Marcus, however, is more unsure of the CARICOM reparations plan as it relates to us as Black British people.

The Ten Point Plan focuses on Caribbean economies and people living in these countries, for obvious reasons, but is silent on how, for instance, Black British people who also suffer racism and the effects of slavery should receive reparations.

As the son of Jamaican citizens this one doesn't actually bother me at all. I am entitled to Jamaican citizenship, as is Marcus (through our respective parents). And most Caribbean countries today have pathways for people of Caribbean heritage to become citizens of their parents or grandparents' respective countries. So, in my mind, reparations that benefit the Caribbean directly and indirectly help me, Marcus and all Black British people descended from enslaved Africans.

Or to put it another way: the vast majority of Black people are only here because the legacy of slavery had destroyed the economies of our parents' countries. The CARICOM plan solves the root of our issues.

The third and possibly the biggest issue is one with which both Marcus and I struggle: where is my cheque? DAMN YOU!!!

We don't mean that in a flippant or greedy way but I still think we personally deserve money for the effects of slavery.

Although I am now more convinced than ever that just giving out money to people like Marcus and me will not solve racism, if the slave owners could be personally 'compensated' for 'losing' their slaves, and we had to personally suffer the indignity of paying them (see Chapter 2), then we should also receive money.

You can do two things at the same time – just look at other examples of reparations in history . . .

9: DON'T MENTION THE WAR

When it comes to the subject of reparations for historical crimes against humanity it's very difficult to discuss those issues without referring to Germany, Israel and the victims of the Holocaust.

I've already mentioned that I'm a fan of *Monty Python's Flying Circus*. Also, that I tend to frame issues through a humorous lens, frequently referencing comedy programmes we all might know and love. In this chapter I am definitely reminded of the *Fawlty Towers* episode 'The Germans' with the recurring punchline 'Don't mention the war!' The entire show revolves around Basil Fawlty doing his utmost not to mention the Second World War (and failing miserably) in front of recently arrived German guests.

The moral of that joke for me – if they can be said to have morals – is that *not* confronting your history only makes matters worse.

No two historical events are ever the same, and to be honest, when Marcus and I have discussed writing about the reparations Germany paid to Israel and to the Jewish victims of the Holocaust we've been nervous about creating false equivalencies or making comparisons that will upset one set of people or another, or both!

At the same time, to write an entire book about reparations and ignore what is probably the most well-known example of reparations in modern history seems ridiculous. If we're going to tackle this issue properly, we need to learn from history, just as much as we ask the people with the power to make reparations to face their own history.

Unlike Basil Fawlty, we need to mention the war.

Interestingly, African Americans started talking about the Nazi war crimes against Jews and drawing parallels to their own situation almost immediately after the Second World War ended.

For example, in 1949 W. E. B. Du Bois, the famous Pan-Africanist civil rights activist, visited the Warsaw ghetto and immediately saw similarities between the Jewish experience and the experiences of the descendants of enslaved Africans in America at the time.

In 1963, the celebrated writer and campaigner James Baldwin drew a direct line between the collective guilt that all white Americans share for the discrimination Black people face and the collective silence of Germans during the Nazi persecution of the Jews.

There is certainly precedent for comparing the two experiences. Marcus and I do believe it is useful to see if there is anything we can learn from other historical examples of reparations, especially when it comes to their implementation.

But for this chapter I am going to hand over to Marcus – not because I am too nervous to write it, but because of personal reasons, I think he might just be better suited to explain the issues. You'll see why. So without further ado.

Over to you, Marcus . . .

◆

Marcus: Thanks Lenny.

If I go back far enough, I have Jewish ancestry, by way of Austria. Although I do not know them personally, I am certain I have relatives – however distant – that were affected by the Holocaust.

I also have a Kenyan wife whose ethnicity is Kikuyu. I married into a family whose members have direct experience of what are known as the Mau Mau uprisings and who were victims of war crimes committed by the British.

The reason I mention my background is because both of these groups, and their experiences, hold important lessons for when we think about reparations. And they help to answer the question at the end of Chapter 8: should we be seeking payment to governments or individuals?

Let's look at the Jewish experience of reparations first.

There is no way a single chapter in this book can give a fully comprehensive account of the Jewish experience of the Holocaust, the German reparations that followed, nor the current Israel–Palestine situation, but my aim here is simply to share some pertinent points that are helpful when thinking about reparations for transatlantic slavery and who should be paid.

When most people think about reparations to the Jewish people for the Holocaust, they start with the Balfour Agreement of 1948 and the establishment of the Israeli state. Alternatively, some people jump ahead to the Luxembourg Agreement of 1952 signed between Israel and West Germany.

I will talk about both, but I will first start a little later, in 1984 when, at the age of thirteen, my attention was drawn by my father to a news story that has stuck with me for over forty years.

The Jewish Experience of Reparations

In April 1984 the then West German Chancellor Helmut Kohl paid a joint visit to the Bitburg cemetery with the then American president Ronald Regan. Buried in the cemetery are various members of the Nazi SS, who were arguably responsible for some of the worst war crimes in history. During the controversy surrounding the visit, the Chancellor remarked that he had the 'mercy of a late birth'. The visit and phrase caused uproar in West Germany because implicit in that short phrase was the belief that he, and anyone born during or after the Nazis came to power, had no responsibility for the actions of the Nazi regime.

While no one thought Chancellor Kohl should take direct responsibility for war crimes committed when he was only a child, it was West German orthodoxy that the nation, as a whole, should take collective responsibility for the Holocaust committed by Nazi Germany, and that collective responsibility included all Germans irrespective of when they were born.

It is fair to say that this news story shaped how I've seen the issue of reparations ever since. If you are members of a nation, and beneficiaries of everything that citizenship of that nation gives you, then you are also responsible for the actions of that nation even if they happened before you were born.

Indeed, after the Second World War, West Germany and its citizens did take responsibility for the war crimes that had resulted in the systematic extermination of 6 million Jews.

The scale of destruction and suffering inflicted upon the Jewish community demanded an equally monumental response in the post-war period. And, as the world grappled with the horrors uncovered in concentration camps, there emerged a consensus on the need for restitution and reparations.

I do not believe it is too controversial to state that this need for restitution and reparation was at the very least partially responsible for the Balfour Agreement of 1948 which established the state of Israel. But I will not even attempt to dip my toe in the troubled waters of the creation of the state of Israel and the ongoing conflict between Israelis and Palestinians. Instead, I will focus on the Luxembourg Agreement of 1952 between West Germany and Israel.

Importantly, for the purposes of this book, the Luxembourg Agreement established how West Germany should pay direct reparations to both another state (Israel) and the individuals who were directly affected by the Holocaust.

In 1952, after extensive negotiations, the Luxembourg Agreement was signed between West Germany and the newly established state of Israel, along with the Conference on Jewish Material Claims Against Germany (Claims Conference), which represented Jewish victims worldwide. This agreement laid the groundwork for what would become one of the most significant reparation efforts in history.

Reparations to the State of Israel

In 1952 the nascent state of Israel faced enormous economic challenges – not unlike the current states in the Caribbean formed out of the transatlantic slave trade. Reparations from Germany were seen as essential for its development and for addressing the needs of survivors.

The Luxembourg Agreement stipulated that West

Germany would pay Israel a sum of 3 billion Deutschmarks over a period of fourteen years. This amount was intended to help integrate Jewish refugees and displaced persons into Israeli society, providing for their welfare and contributing to the economic stability of the nation.

The payments were also used to fund various infrastructure projects, including the construction of housing, industrial plants and transportation networks. This influx of capital played a crucial role in bolstering Israel's economy.

Reparations to Individual Jews

In addition to state-to-state reparations, the Luxembourg Agreement also addressed compensation for individual Jewish survivors of the Holocaust. The Claims Conference, established in 1951, negotiated on behalf of Jewish victims that had suffered persecution, loss of property, and personal injuries under the Nazi regime.

The reparations to individuals took several forms:

1. **Direct compensation payments**
   Germany agreed to make direct compensation payments to individual Holocaust survivors. These payments were meant to provide financial support to those who had lost everything and were often living in dire conditions. The payments varied depending on the level of persecution and loss experienced by the survivors.

2. **Restitution of property**
   Many Jews had their property confiscated or destroyed during the Holocaust. Efforts were made to either return the property to its rightful owners or provide financial

compensation for the losses. This process was fraught with challenges, including bureaucratic hurdles and difficulties in proving ownership, but it was a crucial aspect of the reparations programme.

3. **Pensions and Social Welfare**
For those who had been left with lasting physical or psychological injuries, Germany established pension schemes and social welfare programmes. These programmes aimed to provide a measure of security and dignity to survivors in their old age.

The individual reparations had a profound impact on Holocaust survivors and their descendants. For many, the financial compensation provided a lifeline, helping them rebuild their lives in the aftermath of unimaginable trauma. The pensions and welfare programmes ensured that survivors could live out their remaining years with some degree of comfort.

For the descendants of survivors, the reparations also had a significant impact. In many cases, the financial support helped families achieve a measure of economic stability and pursue educational and professional opportunities that might otherwise have been out of reach. The reparations served as a form of recognition and acknowledgement of the injustices their families had endured.

Important as the Luxembourg Agreement is, it should be noted that the reparations programme it established was part of a broader process of Germany reckoning with its Nazi past. That process included denazification, public trials of war criminals, and the integration of Holocaust education into the national curriculum. It wasn't just financial. And rightly so – as everyone that Lenny and I talk to keeps stressing, financial reparations must be part of a far larger package which should include re-education, and sincere apologies for past actions.

Furthermore, no experts we've read or spoken to think the Luxembourg Agreement was perfect. For instance, it has been criticised for not addressing the psychological harm caused by the trauma of the Holocaust. Other critics have argued that the payments were too small and did not fully address the extent of the suffering endured by Holocaust victims. And the process for individuals to prove they were victims of the Holocaust was far too arduous. If this was the case less than ten years after the Second World War ended, imagine how hard it would be for Black people almost 200 years after slavery ended in the British Caribbean. Finally, the agreement also failed to address the question of reparations for other groups persecuted by the Nazi regime, including Roma, disabled individuals, homosexuals and political prisoners.

But what the Luxembourg Agreement importantly and beautifully illustrates is that there is an historical precedent for any programme of financial reparations to be made to both countries and individuals.

(**Lenny:** So a country like Jamaica can still get everything set out in the CARICOM Reparations Commission's Ten Point Plan *and* I can still get my hot tub? I would just need to prove that my ancestors were enslaved Africans? I'm not sure that is as hard as you might think, Marcus.)
(**Marcus:** OK, I get your point, but before you start picking out colours for your hot tub, I think we should also look at

another example of reparations, one I mentioned at the start of this chapter.)

Reparations to the Kikuyu people

Besides the German reparations to the state of Israel and the Jewish victims of the Holocaust, I would argue that the more recent reparations settlement from the UK government to the victims of British actions against the Kikuyu in Kenya to suppress the Mau Mau uprisings are possibly the next most important in any debate around reparations for the transatlantic slave trade.

For those readers who do not know much about the Mau Mau uprisings and the crimes committed by the British against the Kikuyu here is a brief explainer:

In the early 1950s, Kenya, then a British colony, was experiencing growing discontent among its indigenous population, particularly among the Kikuyu people. The roots of this discontent lay in the economic and social inequalities perpetuated by colonial rule. The fertile highlands had been appropriated by white settlers, displacing many Kikuyu families who were relegated to reserves with poor land and limited opportunities. This led to widespread poverty and frustration.

The Mau Mau movement emerged as a radical response to these grievances. Composed mainly of Kikuyu, but also including members from other ethnic groups, the Mau Mau sought to reclaim their land and assert their rights.

In 1952, the Mau Mau launched an armed rebellion, targeting colonial administrators, settlers and African loyalists. The British response was swift and brutal. A state of emergency was declared, and a massive counter-insurgency campaign was launched. The British employed tactics such as mass detentions, forced relocations and collective punishments. The infamous detention camps, where suspected Mau Mau members were held, became sites of severe torture and inhumane treatment including castration, stinging plants and corrosive substances being forced into the vaginas of women, and children being separated from their families.

The Kenya Human Rights Commission says 90,000 Kenyans were executed. The brutality of the British response is now widely accepted as a crime.

Despite this awful history, Kenya as a country and the survivors of the Kenyan victims of Britain's repression failed to gain recognition and justice for the atrocities they had endured. It wasn't until the early 2000s that the quest by survivors, in particular, gained momentum. In 2009, a group of Mau Mau veterans, represented by the law firm Leigh Day, filed a lawsuit against the British government.

To cut a very long (and heroic) story short, in June 2013, the British government finally announced a settlement. The Foreign Secretary at the time, William Hague, expressed 'sincere regret' for the abuses committed during the Mau Mau uprising and announced a compensation package for the victims – reparations.

The reparations agreement can be roughly divided into three categories:

1. **Financial compensation**
    The British government agreed to pay £19.9 million in compensation distributed among 5,228 Mau Mau veterans, each receiving approximately £3,000.

2. **A public apology**
   Alongside the financial compensation, the British government issued a formal apology. This apology was seen as critical by the survivors as it provided a form of moral acknowledgement and validation of the survivors' experiences.

3. **A memorial fund**
   As part of the settlement, a memorial fund was established to finance the construction of a memorial in Nairobi. This memorial is seen as part of a broader educational tool to inform future generations about this dark chapter in Kenya's history.

I personally think there are several flaws with the British reparations settlement to the Kenyans. For starters, £3,000 to the victims who suffered torture, rape, false imprisonment and bereavements seems tiny to me. Also, the only people that were acknowledged by it as eligible for compensation were the people who directly experienced the British atrocities – not their descendants – and so it meant that some victims died before they were able to receive the monies owed to them. Finally, whenever I talk to my wife's family, and other Kenyans, the idea that only 5,228 people were adversely affected by British colonial rule and deserving of reparations is – to put it diplomatically – laughable.

Despite these shortcomings, I still believe the Mau Mau case holds important lessons and sets crucial precedent when we think about reparations that are due to the descendants of the victims of the transatlantic slave trade.

Specifically, it has five key lessons.

1. **It sets a precedent**

   The British government acknowledged that it was responsible for the crimes committed by previous governments even seventy years later. The case demonstrated that, despite the passage of time, it is possible to seek and achieve justice for historical wrongs.

2. **Apologies are possible**

   Despite what Kenneth Mohammed said about the sincerity of forced apologies (check the last chapter), most people who argue for reparations believe apologies are a critical part of a reparations package.

3. **Re-education is possible**

   The memorial in Nairobi, officially known as 'the Memorial to the Victims of Torture and Ill-Treatment in the Colonial Era, 1952–1960' built within Uhuru Park, which was the venue of the independence speech by Kenya's first leader Jomo Kenyatta in 1963, was a critical step in educating the current and future general population in the realities of the colonial period.

4. **Payment to individuals is possible**

   The £3,000 to individuals was no doubt largely symbolic but it did acknowledge that individuals should personally receive compensation for the crimes committed by the British state and the British people acting with the implicit consent and knowledge of the state.

5. **It serves as an inspiration for other reparation movements**

   The Mau Mau reparations case is thought to have inspired similar movements in other countries. For example, the Herero and Nama people of Namibia have more recently, also successfully, sought reparations from Germany for the genocide committed during the early twentieth century.

Taken together, despite their respective shortcomings, the examples of the German reparations to the state of Israel and the Jewish victims of the Holocaust and the British reparations to the victims of Mau Mau suppression cannot be glossed over. They clearly demonstrate that reparations are not only possible, but essential in redressing historical wrongs.

They also demonstrate that there is no conflict between awarding reparations to individuals and states, both can happen at the same time.

And finally, while £3,000 does not even begin to cover what I believe is really due to individual Kenyans, it would be enough for your hot tub, Lenny.

Lenny: Thank you, Marcus. Now while I think your examples of Israel and the Mau Mau are important, those amounts are chicken feed compared to the trillions of pounds set out by the Brattle Report. Can we ever realistically expect the countries that benefited from transatlantic slavery to hand over trillions? Where will they get that kind of dough?

Marcus: I think I can quote Beyoncé to answer that one. Sorry, I mean Mia Mottley:

We're not expecting that the reparatory damages will be paid in a year, or two, or five because the extraction of wealth and the damages took place over centuries. But we are demanding that we be seen and that we are heard.

Lenny: Not quite as catchy as a Beyoncé lyric, but it does the job. I still think we need to answer the question, though. How can Britain, and the other countries that took part in the transatlantic slave trade, really be expected to pay out trillions?

Marcus: Then I guess it is onward to Chapter 10 . . .

Lenny: (*sings à la theme from* Rawhide . . .) Rollin', rollin', rollin', keep them dogies rollin', Repaaaaaaarations!

10: THE TRILLION-DOLLAR QUESTION (PLUS ANOTHER 20-ISH TRILLION)

'Yes, *but* . . .'

Nearly every discussion I've had about reparations when talking about it with friends and family or colleagues and even publishers has been a 'yes, but . . .' conversation. As Sir Mix-a-Lot might have said back in the day – 'I like "Yes But" and I cannot lie . . .' but I needlessly digress. You know the kind of conversation we're talking about:

'Yes, I agree, slavery is a crime against humanity, but it happened so long ago.'

Or:

'Yes, I think Caribbean countries should get reparations, but I think governments will just misspend all the money.'

Throughout this book, I'd like to think Marcus and I have put all these 'yes, *buts* . . .' to different experts and answered them, or at least put forward an argument that shows that the different 'buts' don't undermine the idea that reparations are not only morally correct but possible.

But there is one 'yes, *but* . . .' that is probably the hardest to answer. It's this one:

'Yes, I agree 100 per cent with the argument for reparations but on a practical level it will never work because where on earth is Britain ever going to find the trillions of pounds it supposedly owes?'

And remember, that's £18.6 trillion to be precise, according to the Brattle Report.

When Marcus and I first discussed writing this book we

thought about not trying to answer this question at all. In doing our research into reparations you would be surprised how many books fail to answer this massive question. The approach seems to be: let's agree on reparations and then let the 'guilty' party worry about where the money comes from – it's not our problem.

That approach was very tempting for us too.

It's just that every time we talked to friends about the book, this 'yes, but . . .' would always come up. We didn't know how to answer, but we also knew that if we didn't tackle it, there would be the same big hole in our book. We even started referring to it as our 'trillion-pound hole'.

And then something literally came to our rescue: a small, possibly unique report published at the end of 2023 entitled 'Making Finance for Reparations and Loss and Damage a Reality: What are the Options?'[1]

It seemed to do exactly what it said on the tin, so Marcus emailed the lead author to see if he would chat to us, and find out whether he really could help us fill our trillion-pound hole.

In life there are two types of clever people. There are the clever people that make you feel really thick by the end of the conversation, and then there are the *really* clever people that make you feel more intelligent by the end of your exchange.

Bhavik Doshi is one of the latter – one of those really, *really* clever people. He is so clever that he makes you feel you could get a PhD if you just had him come round for tea once a week.

Bhavik is an economist turned anthropologist, with undergraduate degrees in economics and postgraduate degrees in development studies and social anthropology. He's worked in banking, finance and economic research, and used to live in Ghana working at a Pan-African tech hub.

He's literally the definition of a renaissance man.

But most importantly for us he led a team of researchers on how to answer the hard question that most people looking at the issue of reparations avoid: how on earth are countries that profited from slavery meant to actually find the trillions of pounds they owe?

The report was commissioned by two organisations: the Advocacy Team, which undertakes policy analysis, political advocacy and campaigning to bring clarity to those important questions that are invariably 'too difficult' for politicians to answer, and Development Reimagined, a consultancy dedicated to bringing fresh perspectives to issues around development, predominantly working with African, Asian and Caribbean governments.

We simply had to talk to Bhavik.

Our first question was the most obvious one: 'Can countries like Britain really afford to pay trillions of pounds?'

Now, before I give you his answer, I want you to know that literally all of Bhavik's answers had an underlying laughter to them. Not a sneering or condescending laugh, but a kind of optimistic, hopeful laugh.

And so, he answered this question with a broad smile and more than a hint of a glint in his eye.

'You're asking the wrong question. The right question is whether the global economic system – which slavery built, and which Britain is fundamentally part of – can afford to pay trillions of pounds to the people and the countries that are owed reparations. And the answer to that is an unequivocal "yes".'

Bhavik then led us through his report step by step.

What he and his team of researchers did first was turn around the question of how countries can afford to pay for reparations. Instead of looking at whether a country has 'enough money in the bank', they looked at how the international financial systems work and whether there are ways to raise the kind of money necessary. In the end, Bhavik identified not just one but fourteen different answers to how countries that currently benefit from a world built on the foundation of the transatlantic slave trade can pay what they owe to countries that are the victims of the slave trade.

We were astounded. It was like getting a free lecture from T'Challa, Tony Stark AND Hank McCoy (three of the brainiest people in the Marvel Universe, doncha know) at once.

Then, the research team scored each answer, or to use Bhavik's language, 'mechanism', against fifteen criteria – like how practical the mechanism might be, or how much money it might actually generate, and so on.

And finally, they suggested a combination of the different financing mechanisms that scored the highest – recognising that we can't put all our eggs in one basket.

For Marcus and me, this was the final 'yes, but . . .' answered. We were elated.

After reading the report, and listening to Bhavik calmly and slowly talking through how it could work, I believe there is no reason why reparations for transatlantic chattel slavery shouldn't become a reality.

So let's go through it now.

One key thing Bhavik did was to identify financial mechanisms already in place that could be ramped up when it comes to transferring large sums of money between countries. In the words of Bhavik, 'Let's look at the wheels that are already there before we invent any new ones.'

I am not going through each of these existing 'big money' transfer mechanisms that the report assessed, but some of the more interesting ones included: debt cancellation relief, long-term government repayments, and something called 'special drawing rights (SDRs) reallocation'.

I worry that I have lost two-thirds of our readers with the word jumble of the last paragraph, which is part of the problem when talking about reparations. Moral and historical arguments for reparations are genuinely interesting, but once you start talking about finance and economics it can become a snoozefest. But Bhavik was able to break down the complicated terms in a way that an educated ten-year-old could understand – which is just about Marcus's and my level of understanding.

He also grounded it in real-life examples.

'Debt cancellation and relief' is pretty much what it says it is . . . It's important because today, many of the countries that are historic victims of the transatlantic slave trade are still heavily indebted to the countries that benefited from that crime. So, a measure that reduces or eliminates the debt owed is a way of effectively transferring money from the creditor country to the debtor country.

There are numerous examples of debt cancellation and relief that were quite popular in the 1990s and 2000s, with many Caribbean and other countries really benefiting from them. For instance, in 2009, the UK wrote off £5 million of debt owed to it by Jamaica. That means today Jamaica doesn't have any outstanding debt to the UK.

Job done?

Well, not so fast. Aside from the fact that Jamaica does have outstanding debt to some big multilateral financial institutions of which the UK government is a shareholder (like the World Bank or the International Monetary Fund), according to Bhavik we should see debt cancellation and relief less as a solution to reparation financing and almost a prerequisite for reparation financing to actually be effective.

Also, as Bhavik explained, while that writing-off on paper might seem like a lovely gift from the UK to Jamaica, historically, creditor countries often imposed conditions on the countries that received debt relief – like making sure they change certain investment policies or trade policies which ultimately benefit the creditor countries. Bhavik was very clear, and we agree, that this goes against the whole nature of reparations, and especially – as we discussed in Chapter 7 – the crucial need for reparations to change the power dynamic between the descendants of the enslaved and the descendants of the enslavers.

For Bhavik, then, debt cancellation is an essential first step. 'If you don't get rid of the current debt, then whatever else you put in place will slowly go to serving that debt.'

Or, to put it in a way that a ten-year-old understands, it's like putting more water into a bucket and not fixing the hole at the bottom first.

So the second mechanism in Bhavik's report that jumped out at Marcus and me was 'long-term government repayments'.

The easiest way to think about this is to go all the way back to Chapter 2, when we wrote about the loan the British government took out to pay compensation to slave owners at the time of abolition.

If you remember, the British government used £20 million to compensate former slave owners under the Slavery Abolition Act of 1833. That £20 million sounds like chump change today but at the time it was the equivalent to approximately 40 per cent of the government's total annual expenditure and 5 per cent of the UK's GDP. So how? Well, the loan that the British government took out to pay for this had a very, very low interest rate and was rolled over into the government's 'gilt' programme – ultimately into an 'undated gilt'.

Again, in language a ten-year-old would understand, the huge £20 million at the time was converted into a debt that would be paid back in the never-never. Indeed, it took almost 200 years to finally pay that debt off.

The fact is, with any debt, if the time frame is long enough and the interest rate on the debt low enough (close to zero) almost no sum is too large.

Finally, there is an existing international financial mechanism that Bhavik talked to us about called 'special drawing rights (SDRs) reallocation'. When Bhavik's report talked about this it exposed just how little most of us understand about how money works on an international level and between countries.

Too often we think of finance in terms of how we deal with our family household finances – but when international economists talk about SDRs I realise household finances and international finances are as different as Newtonian physics (apple falls on Newton's head – BONK!) and Einstein's theory of relativity (What is time? Who is time? Why? WOW, man, that's HEAVY . . . I need a sandwich . . .)

It turns out after the Second World War the International Monetary Fund (IMF) developed a special artificial currency – the SDRs – which all countries can take from the IMF if they have a financial emergency and have no other option. However, to stop everyone doing this all the time for any old excuse, each country is only allowed to take a certain amount every five years. But here is the hitch: some countries are allowed to take more SDRs than others. That means in practice the total SDRs allocated to Caribbean countries are equivalent to just 0.51% of all SDRs in the world, even though they are arguably more likely to run into financial problems, most probably due to the long-term legacy of transatlantic slavery.

Changing the amounts of SDRs that countries can use regularly, and then boosting the total amount of SDRs after this, could give countries of the descendants of slavery literally billions of pounds in a heartbeat. And over time, we could be talking about trillions.

I'll be honest, Marcus and I didn't quite understand it. Does any non-expert really understand Einstein's theory of relativity? Exactly! But you trust physicists to understand and I trusted Bhavik on this one.

But here is the really exciting part of the conversation.

While he was able to walk us through ways in which you do not have to 'reinvent the wheel' to finance reparations, Bhavik's eyes properly lit up when he did 'reinvent the wheel'.

The first idea he talked about was one I had heard before and that was easily Bhavik's favourite: a financial transactions tax (FTT). (Or, as Jamaicans pronounce it: 'FFFFTTTTT! To raatid!')

There have been a few versions of this tax proposed by people looking to redistribute large sums of money and you'll probably recognise the various different names for it including the 'Robin Hood tax' or 'Tobin tax'. I like the Robin Hood name personally, but maybe we need a specific name for it for reparations . . . like the 'Toussaint Louverture tax', in honour of the Haitian revolutionary.

Anyway, the idea is a specific tax on financial transactions where the tax raised is designated for a particular purpose – in this case financing reparations.

The tax would apply to the purchase or sale of things such as stocks, bonds and derivatives, or foreign exchange transactions.

In other words, rich people's tings. And the tax would be a small percentage of the transaction value, applied on both sides of the transaction (buyer and seller).

Although FTTs are not a new concept, in Bhavik's view they come under the category of 'reinventing the wheel' because they haven't ever been implemented on the scale that would be necessary for reparations. The good thing is they come with a tremendous amount of ready-made research, as well as policy and advocacy work that has garnered political support from governments and institutions already. And (we'll get onto this in the next chapter) poll after poll shows the general public support them.

Marcus and I absolutely fell in love with this because it seemed like the only idea that could raise the types of sums the Brattle Report says is owed in reparations.

That said, after talking to Bhavik we had to check what he told us was correct and we hadn't misheard him.

Quoting his report:

> A global FTT placed on all financial transactions (with no exemptions) . . . could generate up to $158 billion per day assuming a 1% tax rate on all trades. There are clear benefits that FTTs provide in that it is quite easily implementable given the advanced nature of the global financial and tax systems. It also allows for funds for reparations to be raised quickly and can directly reduce economic inequality.

Per day? With those types of figures, the £18.6 trillion would actually be possible.

Marcus and I also loved the poetic justice of the FTT idea.

The modern international banking system was literally built off the proceeds of the transatlantic slave trade, and so taxing that system to pay for reparations seemed almost too delightful to be true.

The other idea that really animated Bhavik was 'repurposed financial sanctions'.

The idea behind this one was far more straightforward than the other ideas Bhavik explored, which seemed to require at least ten years of working in the City to fully understand, however simply he explained them. And when he talked about it he leant heavily on the work by the Global Survivors Fund, an organisation set up in 2019 by two Nobel Peace laureates – Denis Mukwege and Nadia Murad – to advocate for reparations for survivors of conflict-related sexual violence around the globe.

The concept behind 'repurposed financial sanctions' is a simple one.

Financial sanctions are often imposed by governments and international organisations to punish other countries or individuals when they are doing something that goes against international norms, or are guilty of a serious international crime.

In the past, the United Nations Security Council has imposed financial sanctions on several countries, including Iran and North Korea. And more recently six G7 countries and Austria imposed sanctions on Russia following the invasion of Ukraine.

Now, this might seem like an old tool – but wait for it. The 'reinvention of the wheel' part of this idea is that normally the sanctions just involve freezing or seizing the guilty country's assets. What the Global Survivors Fund, and Bhavik's report, propose is that these assets don't just sit in some bank somewhere; instead, they're given to people who deserve them in the form of reparations.

Marcus liked this idea because it felt morally right taking assets from a country that had committed an internationally recognised crime and then giving those assets to countries who were the victims of historic international crimes – such as slavery.

For me, there was a risk that it might not have the same neat poetic justice of the Robin Hood tax because – unless transatlantic slavery was then labelled by the United Nations Security Council as an international crime – you might just be taking relatively small amounts of money from countries that might have had nothing to do with slavery to compensate its victims. Now, I am not going to start defending North Korea because they didn't have anything to do with transatlantic slavery. It just feels a bit off to me and would be a very easy way to let countries like Britain and America off the hook.

Bhavik was also worried that this mechanism didn't quite address the fact that the world is not an equal place and that invariably financial sanctions are placed on less powerful countries by more powerful countries.

For example, Bhavik explained that there are some people who would argue that the US should have faced sanctions for invading Iraq just as much as Russia faces sanctions for invading Ukraine. Don't worry, gentle reader, I am not going to attempt to unpick those international political riddles, and Bhavik didn't try to answer his rhetorical question either – he kept smiling – but it did illustrate to us the international political complexities of this solution.

Nevertheless, Bhavik thought repurposing international financial sanctions could work as part of the mix of ways to finance reparations.

And that is the key point.

If you remember, Bhavik's report looked at fourteen different possible mechanisms that could be used to finance reparations.

From the beginning, Bhavik was eager to stress that we shouldn't just think about one silver bullet as being the answer to raising the necessary funds to pay reparations. His view was that we should look at a number of different combinations and monitor how their appropriateness changes over time and from country to country. In other words, we need to have a few strings to our reparations bow.

Now, as I mentioned earlier, the report took all fourteen different financial mechanisms and then rated them against fifteen different criteria.

The judging criteria seemed more complicated than trying to explain the rules of cricket to a Martian. So I won't explain them.

But to cut to the chase – the final conclusion of Bhavik's 108-page report was that a combination of three financial mechanisms would be the most effective.

And they were . . . (drums please . . .)

Debt cancellation, followed by repurposed financial sanctions, plus the Robin Hood tax.

The logic seems to make sense: remove the debt that is constraining countries right now, kick-start the reparations payments with money that has already been confiscated, and then raise the massive sums necessary through an international tax.

When I now hear the 'yes, *but* . . .' about the financing of reparations I can simply say 'yes, *and* . . .'

Thank goodness for clever people like Bhavik!

But let's just add one more thing.

While Bhavik smiled and laughed through our entire chat, he kept stressing two points.

The first one was about the power relationships between people and countries.

If you made a word cloud of the conversation between us the

THE TRILLION-DOLLAR QUESTION

word 'power' was easily the word that came up the most – well, that and the phrase, 'Can you explain that again?'

Whatever solutions and mechanisms you use, Bhavik explained, what we are ultimately talking about is using finance to change international power relationships. That means that the countries and people receiving the money must be in positions of power to decide how it is spent.

Put differently, and drawing on the lessons from how badly debt relief has been done in the past, the view was that, whichever countries are paying the reparations, we must guard against them dictating the terms of how those reparations are given, otherwise it isn't really reparations.

And the second point went right back to the first question we asked him: 'Can Britain afford to pay trillions of pounds?'

At the end of the interview, Bhavik returned to that question. His answer seemed spot on to us.

'It is not a question of whether governments can afford to pay what they owe in reparations. The real question is, do they want to? Is there a political will?'

What we need is a sympathetic politician, with their heart in the right place.

Marcus, you get the van, I'll find night goggles and some duct tape. We're doing this!*

---

* Dear reader – we wouldn't dream of kidnapping a politician, even to get them to at least consider the ideas formulated in this chapter. Honest.

10.5: NOT EVERY DUMPLING MAKES THE SOUP

As we reach the final stretch of our book, Marcus and I want to acknowledge that there were a number of issues around reparations, which we discussed at our Saturday Soup sessions, that didn't make the final cut.

Many of these are important issues that definitely deserve further research and consideration.

But for now, as Marcus likes to say, 'not every dumpling makes the final soup'.

So here is a little insight into the 'discussions' – maybe even 'arguments' – that Marcus and I had around some of the issues that didn't quite get chapters of their own, but were nevertheless important to acknowledge.

Are reparations just about slavery?

Lenny: Marcus, both you and I have Jamaican heritage, and I worry that that has made us lean more towards looking at slavery, rather than other crimes and abuses committed by the British during colonialism.

Marcus: If we are arguing that racism, and the whole construct of race, has its roots in the transatlantic slave trade, I think there's definitely a fair argument that racism owes just as much to European expansion to other parts of the world. Just think of the genocide committed against indigenous people in the Americas.

Lenny: Part two of CARICOM's Reparations Commission's Ten Point Plan is precisely about the genocide committed against the indigenous people in the Caribbean. But when we spoke to Robert Beckford about whether we should think of reparations in a broader context, he said . . . Hold on, I just need to look through my notes . . . OK, got it.

I asked him: 'A lot of people have talked about reparations being not just for slavery, but also about colonialism. What are your views on that?'

He answered, emphatically: 'Slavery only. Colonialism is a different case.'

Also, I think the arguments for reparations for slavery and colonialism are broadly the same. But I do agree with Robert Beckford. Let's just focus on slavery for this book – but I, 100 per cent, want to read a book making the case for reparations for colonialism. I think it's coming.

Should Africans who sold other Africans into slavery be made to pay reparations?

Lenny: Oh, I hate this argument. (*Posh aristo voice.*) 'They're just as bad as each other! Yes, slavery is wrong, but the Africans are just as much to blame as the Europeans, pass the port, Tarquin . . .' Do we really even need to talk about including this in the book?

Marcus: I think we do. The mere fact that you can rattle off the argument means that some people believe it. The argument is out there. If we don't address it, some people will just say we are avoiding the issue.

Lenny: We aren't avoiding the issue. It is just that I really don't think it deserves a whole chapter. This dumpling is definitely not making it into my Saturday soup!

Marcus: I told you you'd start using my phrase eventually!

Lenny: It is a stupid phrase.

Marcus: It might not make a whole chapter but what do you think the argument is against it?

Lenny: All right, in a nutshell – yes, it is a historical fact that certain African leaders and merchants played an active role in the capture and sale of slaves. Those individuals, and even some tribes – if that's the right word – even profited from the trade. BUT, and it is a big but, the reality is the transatlantic slave trade was primarily driven by European demand and facilitated by European traders who provided the infrastructure and market for the trade. You keep talking about looking at power dynamics, and the power dynamics between Europeans and Africans were heavily skewed in favour of the Europeans. Also, African rulers often engaged in the trade under significant duress or as a means of survival in a violent environment, an environment created by Europeans!

Marcus: I agree with you. But before we move on, I do just want to point something out. While European countries today struggle to even issue an apology for the transatlantic slave trade, many African countries have already apologised for the role they played. As part of its fiftieth anniversary independence celebrations in 2006, Ghana included an apology in part of its tourism campaign to welcome Africans in the diaspora back to the country. And, in 1999, the president of Benin apologised to African American clergy for its role in the slave trade.

Lenny: African countries, the victims of colonialism have apologised for the transatlantic slave trade before Britain has?!

Marcus: I think that's what you call 'irony'.

Britain ended the slave trade – should they be rewarded, not made to pay reparations?

Lenny: The fact is Britain was the first European country to abolish the slave trade in 1807, and between 1807 and 1860 the Royal Navy seized approximately 1,600 ships involved in the slave trade and freed approximately 150,000 Africans who were aboard these vessels. Shouldn't that count for something?

Marcus: I do take a bit of issue with the word 'freed', especially as slavery in the British colonies actually continued for another thirty-one years after being 'abolished'. In fact, you know the Africans that were 'freed' by the Royal Navy weren't just taken back home to Africa where they could have a nice life. The vast majority of them were dropped off in the middle of the Atlantic on the island of St Helena.

Lenny: Where Napoleon died?

Marcus: Yes, that St Helena. And they lived in poverty, with thousands of them being buried in unmarked mass graves. It's a really sad story, not a story we should be rewarding or talking about without explaining the full context. There's a brilliant film about it called *A Story of Bones*. Also, several historians argue that the Royal Navy weren't stopping the slave ships of other countries to help Africans – they were doing it to disrupt the trade routes of their rivals.

Lenny: First of all, I need to check out that film. Second, I think you might be being a bit too cynical, Marcus. In our book, we have a lot on the debit side against Britain when it comes to reparations, but we have very little, if anything, on the credit side.

Marcus: I still don't think this dumpling makes the soup.

Lenny: Stop using that phrase!

Marcus: Sorry, I still don't think it deserves a whole chapter. I think if we were to revisit Chapter 6 and the Brattle Report, it might be something we could think about including in the next edition. But I am definitely reminded of Kehinde Andrews' Malcolm X quote on defining reparations: 'Malcolm says that if you stick a knife in my back nine inches, and you only pull it out six inches, that's not progress? Even if you put it all the way out, that's still not progress, you have to heal the wound. And that's what reparations really are.' Ending the slave trade is pulling out the knife six inches, or even just two inches. It isn't reparations.

What are climate change reparations?

Lenny: I'm increasingly hearing people talking about 'climate change reparations'. What are they and are we missing a trick not including them in the book.

Marcus: OK, I know about this because Hannah . . .

Lenny: . . . your wife.

Marcus: Yes, Hannah, my wife, used to be a climate change negotiator at the United Nations and talks about this a lot.

Lenny: I am beginning to think I should have written this book with Hannah and not you.

Marcus: Thanks, Len. Climate change reparations – or what the climate specialists call 'Loss and Damage' because they love to have their own name tags – is a thing. There is even a 'Loss and Damage Fund', being negotiated as we eat our soup.

Lenny: That sounds like a biggie. Why aren't we writing about it?

NOT EVERY DUMPLING MAKES THE SOUP

Marcus: Precisely because it is such a big issue. I don't think you can do it justice in one chapter. There are some brilliant experts on this issue, like Kevon Rhiney from Jamaica who lectures at both Rutgers and Princeton university, who see climate change as being directly related to slavery. There's also a brilliant book that I would recommend called *Reconsidering Reparations* by Olúfẹ́mi O. Táíwò, which frames the whole issue of reparations in terms of 'climate justice'.
Lenny: So one for the next book?
Marcus: Yup, that dumpling is too big for this soup.
Lenny: I'm warning you . . . 'No soup for you!'

11: THE NAME'S LENNY, SPELT WITH A SILENT 'K'

On 25 April 2023, the prime minister at the time, Rishi Sunak, flatly refused to apologise for Britain's involvement in the transatlantic slave trade or to commit to paying reparations.

Yet, just eleven months later, on 25 March 2024, the *Guardian* newspaper ran the headline: 'Six in 10 in UK Poll Say Descendants of Enslaved People Owed Formal Apology'.[1]

Now, I love having Saturday soup with Marcus and discussing difficult and thorny issues around race and Britain's history, but at my age, I ain't got the time or the patience to discuss hypothetical issues just for the sake of it. I've gotta do yoga and the Friday-night big shop. Trust me. It's tough out here in these streets.

So, my big question – which maybe I should have asked even before embarking on writing this book with Marcus rather than at the end – is: will reparations for the transatlantic slave trade ever become a reality?

I know, as we've already written, that there are examples of individuals such as Laura Trevelyan paying reparations, and companies paying what they believe they owe, such as the *Guardian* and Lloyd's of London. But as we argued in Chapter 7, these are not the kind of reparations that we believe will truly transform society.

To achieve that transformation, we need reparations to come from the state. The men and women at the top level, the muckety-mucks, the lords and ladies of all they survey – and that means looking at our government, specifically the British government.

So, I sent an email to the politician who had asked the question Rishi Sunak responded to by saying he would not apologise for Britain's role in transatlantic slavery. I had one simple question: 'Am I wasting my time?'

Bell Ribeiro-Addy is the Labour MP for Clapham and Brixton Hill. This constituency is significant in UK history for being one of the most important areas for the modern Black British community following the Second World War.

Ribeiro-Addy entered the UK Parliament in December 2019 and in her maiden speech in the House of Commons raised the issue of reparations.

Almost two years later, in November 2021, she helped establish the Afrikan Reparations All-Party Parliamentary Group bringing together 'parliamentarians, campaigners, communities, and other stakeholders to examine issues of African reparations and the repatriation of art and cultural artefacts, as well as exploring policy proposals on reparations and development, and how best to redress the legacies of African enslavement and colonialism'. It is a group she now chairs.

And less than two years after its establishment, in 2023, the group organised the first ever UK reparations conference.

It's fair to say Ribeiro-Addy is a relentless and active person. And if anyone was going to be able to tell me whether reparations will ever become a reality, this was the person.

Interestingly, when she asked Rishi Sunak if he would apologise for Britain's role in slavery and raised the issue of reparations, her own party was not quite on the same page as she was. At the time, a Labour spokesperson issued a statement that subtly distanced itself from her question to Sunak, saying Ribeiro-Addy 'is right to highlight the appalling history of the slave trade', but adding, 'On the specific point of reparations, the point that she was making is not Labour Party policy.' (Teflon shoulders, you gotta love 'em.)

In fact, in the UK, the Green Party is – at the time of writing – the only major political party that has an official policy when it comes to reparations. Their policy is to 'establish a Parliamentary Commission of Inquiry for Truth and Reparatory Justice to address reparations needed to redress global inequalities caused by the transatlantic trafficking of enslaved Africans'. And while this is not quite a policy that says the Green Party would actually support reparations after a Commission of Inquiry report, even so, in terms of reality, the party only has four MPs in the UK Parliament. With numbers like that I don't think they will be able to implement even this commission any time soon, at least not on their own.

So when Marcus and I finally spoke to Ribeiro-Addy, I asked her: does she think reparations will ever become a reality?

I was incredibly surprised at how upbeat she was.

First of all, she seemed to agree with a lot of the previous experts and leaders we'd spoken to that reparations are critical to 'solving racism once and for all'. She told us: 'If you're really trying to tackle what the problem is, you're looking at the root cause, and the root cause of a lot of the racism that we face today is quite literally in the transatlantic slave trade and the colonialism that followed afterwards . . . and if we're going to look at making changes, repairing that imbalance that has come about, we have to look at reparations.'

However, when I asked her if reparations were really going to happen, she was quick to emphasise the need to not see reparations as just one policy but as a series of different policies.

Like almost everyone else we have spoken to for this book, she was also quick to stress the need to 'go beyond just financial payments'.

For example, taking just one part of reparations, the need for better education around Britain's role in the transatlantic slave trade, Ribeiro-Addy pointed out that UK parliamentary petitions on the need to teach Black history in schools receive more signatures from the British public than any other issue.

She then went on to compare the issue of reparations to how some women's or LGBTQ issues were viewed just twenty or thirty years ago.

'I think when reparations are better explained to people – what we mean by reparations – you'll find that people are more receptive to it. There was a time that people thought that women's rights or talking about race at all couldn't be a vote winner, or LGBTQ rights couldn't be a vote winner. Now, if you have some really awful views on women's rights or LGBTQ rights, you're not the type of individual that would probably get elected in Parliament.'

Marcus used to be a senior news executive at the BBC, so when he heard her say that, he couldn't help himself from interrogating her a little further. 'Do you really see reparations as being akin to women getting the right to vote or gay people getting the right to marriage equality? Do you honestly think we'll look back on reparations in ten years' time and see it like that?'

Bell Ribeiro-Addy just smiled at Marcus the way a parent does to a small child asking if Santa Claus is really going to give them everything on their Christmas list. 'I hope so. And I definitely don't see why not. I mean, they're all different liberation struggles. And they're all ones which presumably caused controversy in their time. But they are all about the advancements of particular groups of people. And people in time came to see they were needed. So I'm hopeful.'

The difference, in my humble opinion, is that women make up over 50 per cent of the population, and while people might have been ideologically opposed to marriage equality it didn't actually cost them anything.

So we can dance around the edge of reparations and pick off the issues – such as Britain making a formal apology for the slave trade, or the need for better understanding and education around the issue – but ultimately for reparations to work there must actually be a financial component. The non-financial aspects of reparations are necessary, but they're not sufficient without the money.

Would the British public really ever vote for giving substantial amounts of money to the descendants of the victims of the transatlantic slave trade? Surely, this would be against the interests of any British government?

Ribeiro-Addy definitely sees the issue of reparations for the transatlantic slave trade and reparations for colonialism as being part of the same struggle and had a very pragmatic answer to this point.

'People think that when I talk about reparations, they say, "How could you as a British MP just want to take things away from the UK?" But the reality is I'm actually thinking about Britain's self-preservation.

'I think about how India has made progress in so many different ways; the same is true for so many former UK colonies in Africa which are also advancing. And if we're not careful, all of these countries will advance *in spite* of what's been done to them . . . and not because we've done anything to help address atrocities of the past. And when that happens, people in those countries will look at us and say, "Remember what the UK did to us?" Meaning that when it comes to trade deals, when it comes to all these different things, the UK will be at the back of the queue.

'Every country needs allies, and we're just not going to have any allies.'

Reparations as self-enlightened foreign policy was an argument that neither Marcus nor I had heard before. For this book we'd been so focused on what reparations can do for us, as Black people within the UK, that we hadn't stopped to think what reparations could do for white people and nations which had benefited from the transatlantic slave trade.

This was one of those lightbulb moments for us. PING!

But Ribeiro-Addy didn't stop there.

'I think it [reparations] serves a dual purpose. Governments have a duty to display the morality of their citizens across the world, and British morality is important. But reparations are also important for the UK's future survival. I don't want the UK to be looked on as a hated country. I want our standing in the world to be one that is respected and viewed in a very positive light, in a way that means no one will attack us, no one will look badly upon us.'

And then came the line that summed it all up in eight words.

'Reparations will help us be a better country.'

I cannot tell you how energised Marcus and I felt at this point talking to Bell Ribeiro-Addy. Neither of us are party political animals so I am not going to start campaigning for any party, but at that moment I think if Bell had decided to set up her own party and run for prime minister, she would have had my vote.

I had to push it just that little bit further. Whilst I completely understand that reparations is so much more than just finances,

I was curious – did she think I will actually get any cash in my hand in my lifetime? After all, the title of this book is *The Big Payback*.

And to my dismay the answer was: 'I don't think you should count on getting a cheque any time soon.' (In my mind's eye, all those fifty-pound notes took flight with wings, and soared off into the distance, like in an old *Tom and Jerry* cartoon. Dang . . . I guess I don't get no hot tub . . .)

In fact, she doesn't think personal cheques should be the focus of any reparations policies.

'I think cheques are not necessarily going to change things. Actually, this point goes right across any racial lines. If you gave somebody who has grown up rich a million pounds, someone who is tied into all of the existing structures, and you gave somebody who has grown up working class a million pounds, and you came back five years later, you would find that the working-class person has probably depleted it quite a bit, whereas the rich person who has grown up around wealth may have tripled it, quadrupled it, for the simple fact that they are used to having money, and they are used to the institutions that grow and maintain and protect the money.'

I could see Marcus bristle at what he thought was the paternalistic – and possibly condescending – nature of Ribeiro-Addy's view. Although, throughout the book I've been the one who has been asking about the cash I might receive due to reparations and Marcus has been far more focused on the bigger issues, I could see that the very idea that poor Black people wouldn't know what to do with their reparations money rankled.

But then Ribeiro-Addy elaborated, swiftly easing what I tease Marcus about as his radical left-wing student concerns: 'I think we need to get away from the idea of just handing over money without changing structures. Some of those are national structures and some of those are global structures.'

Ribeiro-Addy's argument against handing over money was not just about handing over money to individuals, it also held true with regards to governments as well.

'We're going to find a situation where the imbalance remains simply because the country [that receives reparations money] has never had the tools to maintain its wealth. So, when it comes to reparations I'm talking about the way in which the IMF (International Monetary Fund) works, the way in which even the UN works by having a Security Council which has no [permanent] representation of any Black majority country on it . . . All of these things, all of these international structures are there literally to keep people in what's known as the "Global South" down. And if you give them money without changing those structures, all that will happen is they will end up spending money from Western companies. And then that imbalance remains. So until we change certain structures, I just don't think simply writing cheques is going to make a difference.'

Or to put it another way – if I want to buy a hot tub with my reparations money, let's make sure there are Black businesses that are selling hot tubs that I can choose from. And with the money left over, let's make sure I have the choice to put it in a bank that isn't steeped in the history of the transatlantic slave trade. Maybe even a bank that is set up and run by the descendants of enslaved Africans. People who look like me and Marcus, but just have better maths skills.

Talking to Bell Ribeiro-Addy about reparations felt like a horrible episode of *Who Wants to be a Millionaire?* where Chris

Tarrant puts the cheque in your hand only to whip it away again.

'But I don't wanna *give* you that . . .'

The British public already supports reparations . . . *but* only the parts that don't involve handing over money.

The British government might not support reparations now . . . *but*, like the struggle for marriage equality or women's rights, this could literally change overnight.

It is completely in the UK's long-term self-interest to support reparations . . . *but* if it handed over any money now it could just entrench existing power imbalances.

For the rest of the conversation Ribeiro-Addy talked across a range of issues – from the need to 'decolonise' UK aid to building the financial institutions and industrial structures of former British colonies. She also shared her views on the policies of the IMF that she feels have effectively kept countries in the Caribbean and Africa in poverty, and the non-governmental organisations (NGOs) that have ploughed billions into 'development' with few tangible results when it comes to changing African or Caribbean countries' position relative to the 'West'.

Yet, at the end of the conversation Marcus and I were strangely optimistic.

Despite Ribeiro-Addy's own pessimism, I do believe reparations could happen in my lifetime. But the task ahead of us to achieve them is far larger than either of us had ever realised before we started writing this book.

So the last, and final, question we put to ourselves as we finished speaking to Bell Ribeiro-Addy and thought about our next chapter was: *what can we do personally to make it happen?*

SPELT WITH A SILENT 'K'

Marcus: Lenny, I think you forgot one thing! Why does the Afrikan Reparations All-Party Parliamentary Group, which Bell Ribeiro-Addy, MP, chairs, spell Africa with a 'k'?

Lenny: Thanks, Marcus – let's leave the last word to Bell:

> The 'k' is meant to signify that we are talking about peoples of African descent, wherever they might be in the world. Some people don't like to call themselves 'Black'. Some people don't like to call themselves 'Black British', or 'African American', or 'XYZ'. But one thing that we can all say is those people that specifically suffer from the after-effects of slavery and colonialism are those that came from Africa. And when we're talking about them, and we're talking about reparations, and talking about it holistically, we use the 'k' to make sure that people are clear that it's not just people on the African continent we are talking about, we're talking to people in the Caribbean, we're talking about people in the US. Black Britons. And across the rest of Europe.

12: WHAT NEXT?

And . . . exhale!

You, dear reader, have finished the book, and Marcus and I have completed our research into reparations.

This chapter is what would normally be the 'conclusion', but for us it seems more fitting to title it 'What Next?' Because if we believe in everything we have just written, we can't just finish here.

At one point the working title for this book was *Everything You Wanted to Know About Reparations but Felt too White to Ask*. I know – it's a bit of a mouthful. *The Big Payback* is a lot better.

But for Marcus and me, the working title – a little tongue-in-cheek – summed up what we were trying to achieve. Reparations is one of those things that far too many of us talk about but far too few of us actually understand.

And all too often we are too scared to ask questions about reparations for fear of showing our ignorance or even offending someone. The problem with the working title – apart from it being far too long – is that this fear (of exposing your ignorance or offending someone) applies to Black and white people alike. At least, I know I was fearful before embarking on this book, and I think Marcus felt the same way.

People told us we would become targets of the right-wing media for even talking about Britain's role in the transatlantic slave trade, let alone the idea that Britain still has a responsibility and duty to rectify the historical wrongs committed during slavery.

WHAT NEXT?

Then, as we delved deeper into the issues, we were worried that the left-wing press might come gunning for us for suggesting that well-meaning liberals – both individuals and organisations – attempting to atone for the wrongs of their ancestors is 'not really reparations', or even that no one is getting a cheque in the post.

But we have tried our best to be intellectually honest and open, and we have tried to be as transparent as possible as to how and why we have reached the conclusions we have reached.

You, as the reader, may come to different conclusions, and form different views on the merits (or otherwise) of reparations. But at least now we hope you have enough information to engage with the issue with some knowledge – and we can start to have a debate.

And we should never be afraid of having a debate. It is way past time that we started to seriously debate reparations.

Overcoming that fear and following my intellectual curiosity is one of the best decisions I have made in a long time, and I am so glad that Marcus came along for the ride – frequently taking over the steering wheel.

What began as a small research project for me into an issue that piqued my interest, and which I wanted to write a play about, has turned into one of the most important things I believe Marcus and I have done together in the last ten years. This book has been an education for me in what we both believe is the most important issue in the world today.

Ironically, in writing this conclusion to a book about reparations, I have to admit that what I've come to realise is that this book is actually less about reparations than about the origins of racism and how we solve the fact we live in a world of racial inequality that must end.

That racial inequality manifests itself over and over again, fuelled both by direct racism, indirect racism and historic racism that has embedded injustices that have not been addressed and rectified.

We see that racial inequality in Britain through facts such as:

1. For every £1 white British households hold in wealth, Black Caribbean people hold just 20p and Black African just 10p.[1]
2. Black British people are twice as likely to be unemployed than our white counterparts.[2]
3. The number of Black professors in UK higher education institutions represent just 1 per cent of all professorial staff.[3]
4. Black British people are seven times more likely to die after being restrained by the police compared to our white counterparts.[4]
5. Black women in the UK are four times more likely to die in pregnancy and childbirth than white women.[5]
6. Black British people are more than three times as likely to experience homelessness than our white counterparts.[6]
7. In parts of England, exclusion rates are five times higher for Black Caribbean pupils compared to their white counterparts.[7]
8. Far too many of us still experience direct racial abuse with 40–50 per cent of Black British people reporting having experienced racial abuse while just going about our daily business while out shopping, in parks, cafes or restaurants, or on public transport.[8]
9. On average almost a quarter (23 per cent) of Black British people will experience a common mental health problem in any given week – higher than any other racial group in Britain.[9]
10. Black British people are twice as likely to have symptoms relating to post-traumatic stress disorder compared to our white British counterparts.[10]

WHAT NEXT?

But what a book about reparations tells us is that this is not just about solving racism in Britain. The transatlantic slave trade laid the foundations, at least partially, for an entire world built on racism.

Globally, we see racial inequality manifest itself today with facts such as:

1. No Black majority country has a permanent seat on the UN Security Council.[11]
2. Six of the eight countries that make up the G7 directly benefited from the transatlantic slave trade. Not one country that was the victim of the transatlantic slave trade is a member.[12]
3. The Caribbean is one of the poorest regions of the world[13] with approximately 32 per cent of people[14] in Latin America and the Caribbean living below the poverty line.
4. Racism and racial inequality against the descendants of enslaved Africans can be seen in almost all white majority countries.
5. The total GDP of the Caribbean countries (CARICOM, to be precise) is approximately a tenth of the GDP of the Netherlands, which has a history of transatlantic slavery and less than half the population of the Caribbean and few natural resources in comparison.

I could continue listing fact after fact highlighting racial inequities, both in Britain and globally, and while some people may want to pick holes in one or two specific examples, I do not believe it is at all controversial to say that the world is a racially unequal place today.

If we do not believe people of African descent are somehow inherently inferior to white people, if we do not believe the communities and countries of the descendants of the enslaved are inherently inferior to the descendants of the communities and countries that benefited from the transatlantic slave trade, and if we do not believe that there is something inferior in the DNA of people who are racialised as Black versus the DNA of people who are racialised as white . . . then these differences must be due to the effects of racism – past and/or present.

In 2020, when the Black Lives Matter protests swept the globe, we saw a real desire across the world to acknowledge and address the racial inequalities I listed above – and many more. A real appetite to re-examine the understanding of our histories and the role race plays in our lives.

We were told this was going to be the 'generation to end racism'.[15]

We saw companies post black squares on their social media accounts in solidarity with the struggles that Black people face in fighting racism.

And national football teams took the knee to demonstrate that they were not just 'not racist' but they were actively 'anti-racist'.

But in the years that have followed, we have seen high-profile British politicians stand on platforms that in my opinion are positively racist.

We have seen policies in the US to address racial inequality, such as affirmative action, rolled back.

We have seen the rise of the far right across Europe with the election of an Italian prime minister who praised the fascist Mussolini when she was a teenager.

And we saw racist anti-immigration riots sweep the UK in 2024.

While this book is ostensibly about reparations, in reality it is about 'solving' racism, addressing the causes of racism, and empowering people to fight racism whenever it appears.

Increasingly, as Marcus and I have written this book, we have come to the conclusion that reparations are the only way to address these issues and 'solve' racism once and for all.

If reparations are to fulfil the goal of repairing the damage done by the transatlantic slave trade then, by definition, that must mean ridding the world of racism.

If you believe, like us, that the modern world is built on the foundations, at least partially, of the transatlantic slave trade, then reparations must dismantle those foundations and finance the making of new foundations.

We must dismantle the foundations which meant that when there was a global pandemic African and Caribbean countries were at the back of the queue in receiving vaccines and non-white people in the UK were disproportionately affected.

I no longer think that the concept of reparations is about simply giving people like me, or people who look like me, a pay cheque. Any more than it would have been about giving my enslaved ancestors a pay cheque when they were freed, without realising that their former enslavers still owned all the companies and plantations they could work for and spend all their money at.

And, possibly controversially, while large organisations can and should make amends for their participation in the slave trade, I no longer see this as 'reparations'.

At best this would be the equivalent of a sugar plantation owner in the 1800s freeing all their slaves – and even paying them money – but freeing them into a world where slavery was still legal. The plantation owner is definitely doing the right thing – and should be commended for it – but freeing Africans into a world beset with slavery is not going to solve racism.

This is by no means criticising all the organisations who have made massive steps, implementing anti-racism policies and paying large sums of money in the name of reparations. But we need a new name for this, maybe 'slavery compensation' or 'racial reckoning' or 'restorative justice' (which the *Guardian* has used).

This is no doubt doing the right thing, but for me it falls short of what we are trying to achieve when we talk about reparations. The actions of individuals and companies cannot, by themselves, change the way the world works. Right now, from the British education system to the United Nations, we can see how world systems favour the descendants of the slave owners and work against the descendants of the enslaved.

A simple transfer of money is not going to do it. Especially at the relative levels that those transfers are happening right now.

Fundamentally, and at its very essence, reparations must be about power and its redistribution.

Money and finances are often a proxy for power and can be empowering, but giving money alone is just compensation; giving people power is the real 'repair' in reparations.

Reparations is about repair and changing how power is shared within countries and between countries.

I know changing the world sounds like a tall order and something that we can't do, but I believe we can and must.

I believe we have demonstrated that the logical and moral argument for reparations is unassailable.

I believe we have shown that there have been cases where reparations have not only been implemented, but have worked.

And, lastly, I believe that we have shown that, with the political will, we can raise the finances to make reparations a reality.

WHAT NEXT?

It is not going to be easy but there are five things I believe we can all do today to get a little bit closer to making it happen.

So the last question of the book must be: what can we do – especially here in the UK?

WHAT CAN WE DO?

1. **Write to your local MP**
   Reparations are political and will only become a reality if our government has the political will to make them work. Let it know your views on what you think Britain's role should be in making reparations, as well as what the UK can do at home and internationally to make them a reality.

2. **Support research into the transatlantic slave trade and its legacy**
   Support bodies such as the Centre for the Study of the Legacies of British Slavery (ucl.ac.uk/lbs), based at University College London – CSLBS is the UK's leading public history centre for research on the history of slavery and its aftermath.

3. **Support CARICOM's Ten Point Plan for reparations**
   As individuals we can do this by simply telling people about it, making sure it is more widely known in the UK.

4. **Support organisations that help the descendants of the transatlantic slave trade**
   There are many such organisations: two examples are the Stephen Lawrence Day Foundation (stephenlawrenceday.org), which addresses racial inequality in the world of architecture, and the Pepper Pot Centre (pepperpotcentre.org.uk) in North Kensington, London, which helps elderly people in the British Caribbean and African community.

WHAT CAN WE DO?

5. Never stop believing
One day racism will be a thing of the past – we cannot give up hope.

Together we can make the world a better place. We just need to keep our eyes on the prize.

THE BIG PAYBACK: THE PLAY

A NOTE FROM LENNY

The following piece of work was written during the process of Marcus and me developing and then revising *The Big Payback*. I wanted to humanise the issue of reparations, rather than just academically poke at them with a stick. I've found throughout my career that the best way for me to learn is by doing – therefore, creating a group of characters in order to debate the pros and cons of giving or receiving reparations felt like an excellent way to navigate this thorny path. Obviously, I didn't just want people arguing in an enclosed space; I also wanted a sense of location – from New York to London to Scotland to Acocks Green. Emotionally I felt that, for our protagonist, there would be immense guilt, self-doubt and prevarication – all the feelings that can occur when a decent person considers doing the right thing. There was also the sense that there be a number of viewpoints and voices. Ranging from 'Give us all your money!' to 'It's not just about the money!' to 'I take this personally and I want to make some kind of amends – please allow me to do that for you,' all the way to 'This concerns your ancestors, hundreds of years ago. You should just go and live your life and forget about us and reparations.'

There's a reason Saturday soup features in the play. As I was writing, and the characters began arguing about the issue, I felt a connection. The whole thing felt like the times Marcus and I were eating Saturday soup and going back and forth, hammer and tongs, over the issues. Often, the best place for debate is round the dinner table – we all do it, all the time. So why wouldn't our hero be invited to Birmingham, eat big food, and find himself hip-deep in an almighty row about whether he should give the descendants of his forefathers' slaves a humungous cheque?

Aaron Sorkin (author of *The West Wing* and *A Few Good Men*) writes about all drama being about just two things: intention and obstacle. Every character must have something they want and seemingly insurmountable obstacles in the way of achieving them.

Our hero's desire in the play is simple: 'Do I take responsibility for my ancestors' actions? What shape does that responsibility take?' The obstacles are: his management, the broadcasters of his TV show, his family, preserving his reputation as a nice guy, and much more.

I'm not sure there are any concrete resolutions – but we do what we can do, right?

SIR LENNY HENRY
FEBRUARY 2025

THE SCRIPT

Characters

Shelton Braddock
A delivery driver (Black, fifties)

Delyse Braddock
His wife (Black, fifties)

Amelia Braddock
Their daughter, a teacher (Black, thirties)

Glenroy Braddock
Their son, a basketball player (Black, twenties)

Jack Braddock
An actor (white, thirties)

Dane Brown
An actor (Black, thirties)

Anthony Webber
Jack's agent (white, forties)

Winn Grant
Forensic MDs director (white, fifties)

Annie Clayton
A documentary director (mixed race, thirties)

Colette Murchison
A professor at Columbia University (Black, thirties)

Duncan Logan
A herald from the College of Arms

| **A runner** | **A cameraman** | **A sound guy** |
| (white, twenties) | (Black, thirties) | (white, thirties) |

Notes

The stage is a black box at first.

As lights come up, we see a large screen at the back of the stage.

The set is multipurpose and adaptable.

Our supporting cast will delight us with their physical and dialectal versatility.

1. THE BRADDOCKS' LIVING ROOM, ACOCKS GREEN

The Braddock family's house is modern British Caribbean and working class. A mixture of flock wallpaper, books and records everywhere. Antimacassars on the sofa – plastic paths on the carpet for cleanliness purposes.

Shelton Braddock (Black, fifties) is sitting on the sofa with his son, Glenroy (Black, twenties).

On their big screen telly are the opening credits of: 'Forensic MDs'.

Glenroy has his feet on the table (one of his knees is in plaster). Shelton chastises him.

Shelton Glenroy, boy, move yu foot – they stink.

Glenroy I put Febreze on them this morning.

Shelton That was this morning – now it's tonight – an' dem still stink!

Glenroy's mum, Delyse (Black, fifties), enters with snacks.

Glenroy (*mock upset*) Mum, he's having a go at me about work again.

Delyse The boy's had a terrible injury, Shelton – why you can't leave him alone?

Shelton 'Terrible injury' my arse – boy gets lickle tap on his kneecap and can't ever go back to work?

Delyse Give it a rest nuh, Shelton? You're exhausting.

Glenroy Shhhh.

On screen: a good-looking Dr Zach Johnson (white, thirties) appears; a credit says he's played by: 'Jack Braddock'.

Delyse Look at Dr Zach, nuh? He's so good-looking. (*takes him in*) I could eat him with a spoon.

Shelton Delyse – that's disgusting. Calm yourself.

Delyse You calm yourself. Look at him – all blonde and handsome with his lickle abdominal muscles dem.

Glenroy He's wearing surgical scrubs, Mum, you can't see his muscles.

Delyse I can see them in my mind.

Shelton You need to stop this foolishness – you could hurt my feelings.

Delyse I been married to you for thirty years – what about my feelings?

On screen: a still of Dr Jaheim Yashere (Black, thirties) appears. A credit says: 'Dane Brown'.

Shelton *I* hurt *your* feelings? When?

Delyse Every time you open your mouth.

Shelton Well, that's not fair.

Glenroy You two shush! Dr Jaheim's gonna say it . . .

On screen: Jaheim and Zach look down into a body cavity.

Jaheim (*on TV*) Man . . . I can't belieeeeve this shit!

Glenroy has joined in with this line.

Zach (*on TV*) We're gonna need a bigger scalpel.

Jaheim's reaction and then:

Delyse It's pure foolishness but I love it.

Glenroy Shush – Dr Zach's gonna talk about responsibility and medicine and stuff.

On screen: Jaheim and Zach operate on a patient – they talk as they go.

Zach (*on TV*) Our job is to take responsibility for the patient; our motto: Do no harm.

Jaheim (*on TV*) My motto is: Get paid . . . by any means necessary.

Zach (*on TV*) You don't mean that.

Jaheim (*on TV*) Your parents are rich, you're a surgeon – my parents were lower working class – so if you don't mind? Imma sell organs –

They argue on screen as:

Delyse How is he allowed to say that?

Glenroy Shhhh! They gotta remove a brain tumour.

The door opens. It's Glenroy's sister, Amelia (Black, thirties).

Amelia! It's on! Grab your weirdo tea and let's get stuck in.

But Amelia's just stood there looking at them over the sofa.

Delyse You all right, Amelia? How was school today?

Amelia I'm fired.

Delyse / Shelton / Glenroy Lord God / Backside! / Whaaaat?

On screen: stay with Zach and Jaheim.

2. JACK'S TRAILER

Jack Braddock is sitting in his surgeon's costume; knocking back an energy shake, he opens his computer.

On the large screen: his LA agent, Anthony Webber (white, forties), appears, rocking the power suit and a ton of attitude. He loves Jack, though, and that comes across.

Anthony Jackie, baby, sweetheart, bubbeleh! How they hanging?

Jack (*light Scottish*) Anthony, please. We've talked about this: You're not Jewish!

Anthony Tell that to my rabbi. My foreskin's in the mail.

Jack Ugh.

Anthony (*a beat*) Enough small talk, boychick! It's your third year on *Forensic MDs*! Ratings? Very respectable. You're a global sex symbol! AND I got an upgrade: asked for seven figures for you per episode next year . . . they agreed . . . So. Cue applause . . . (*a beat*) Are you in?

Jack studies Anthony's focused face for a moment.

Jack (*thinks*) I don't know, Anthony; I've been thinking about this stage adaptation of those Chekhov short stories for George at that warehouse theatre in Brooklyn.

Anthony inhales and then:

Anthony Are you shitting me? They're talking seven figures an episode and you wanna ditch that for Chekhov? (*Chekhov acting*) 'Medicine is my lawful wife, and literature is my mistress.'

Jack (*laughing*) I love it when you do Chekhov. Of course I'm in, I'm loving it.

Anthony Thank God. OK – so I'll set up the deal memo toot sweet. Oh, I got a call from this documentary maker in London; she's in love with you, the way she was talking to me.

Jack You pimping me out to a documentary maker? What is this?

Anthony No!!! If I was pimping you, I'd be broke in a week. She wants you for this show, *Celebrity DNA*. You spit into a tube – then, two weeks later they know who your ancestors were in Jurassic times. I haven't seen it myself, but I've heard it's delightful.

Jack Sounds a bit like *Who Do You Think You Are?*

Anthony This digs a little deeper than that show. These scientists work alongside historians who trace your ancestors forensically. Director's name is Annie Clayton. She worked at the BBC. She's good.

Jack I'm sure she is, but if she's looking to muckrake, my Scottish Presbyterian family are dead boring. I mean, I've never really known my family's origins. (*thinks*) I've got to find something about me that's interesting for my next dinner party. Maybe I'm related to Braveheart?

Anthony Exactly. The more we peel the onion of Jack Braddock, the more saleable you are.

Jack Well, I'm convinced. Let's do it – here's to peeling my onion.

Anthony She's arriving today. (*looking past Jack*) Don't you have work to do?

Dane puts his head around the door; he affects a terrible Scottish accent.

Dane (*bad Scottish accent*) Big man? Ye ready to start filmin' the noo? (*Connery*) 'My name is Bond.'

Jack glares at him, then to his screen:

Jack Anthony, I must go, my friend Dane is attempting to kill me with Scottish.

Anthony (*waves at the screen*) Tell your friend his accent needs to be stabbed with a fork until it's dead.

Dane gives the screen the finger, but Anthony's gone.
Jack laughs.
They laugh and are then interrupted by a runner (*white, twenties*), *who puts his head round the door:*

Runner Annie Clayton – the documentary woman's asking for you two on set.

Jack She's an award-winning director. She's not just 'documentary woman'. Show some respect.

Dane Yeah, she's won like six big-ass awards so yeah – show some respect, amigo.

Pause.

Jack / Dane Pulling your leg! / Just funnin!

Jack Obviously in ten years' time when you're running Apple TV, you'll forget this moment ever happened.

The runner looks scared.

Jack Shall we?

Dane Wakanda for ever!

They cross their arms in the Wakanda salute and exit.

3. OPERATING-ROOM SET

Back on the set of Forensic MDs. *A brisk and confident director, Annie Clayton* (*mixed race, thirties*), *roams the set rearranging camera positions and looking through a viewfinder. Jack's there too – waiting for something to happen. Then:*

Annie Lovely. Nice contrast between our light and theirs. OK, this is good. This is excellent.

She looks at her cameraman (white, thirties), who gives the thumbs-up. She flashes Jack a hundred-kilowatt smile.

Annie So, Jack, just be natural. You'll begin like we practised and then we'll get on to the bit about the DNA test. Ready?

Jack nods. Jack's in close-up on the big screen behind.

All right, in three, two, one. Action.

Jack (*inhales*) Hi, I'm Jack Braddock. My friend Dane Brown and I play two young surgeons in the hit *Forensic MDs*. 'Solving medical mysteries in real time!' *Variety* said: 'It's *Suits* with scalpels!' Today, though, I'm here to drool into a tube for *Celebrity DNA*!

Annie So tell us what you know about your bloodline, Jack . . .

Jack OK, so – I'm of Scottish heritage.
My parents are from near Loch Fyne.
That's where I grew up, went to school.
I studied drama in London; waited tables; went for loads of auditions. I was a White Walker in *Game of Thrones*. (*moans/laughs*) I really wanted to be a treacherous goblin in *The Witcher* but, apparently, I wasn't treacherous enough. Then I read for *Forensic MDs* and it changed my life immediately.
Anyway, I digress. I believe someone called Colette is going to extract fluids from my body. But in a proper way. Y'know – not like – Ah, jeez, can we redo that?

Annie It's already erased. She's not a 'someone', she's a professor: one of Columbia University's finest. Come on, Colette.

Colette (Black, thirties) is very nervous (and completely starstruck). She unpacks the equipment for the DNA test and instructs Jack on what to do.

Jack My bad.

Colette No problem, Mr Braddock. Now, if you wouldn't mind releasing some saliva into the test tube and then sealing the sample with the lid, making sure it's really tight there . . .

Jack spits into the tube, corks it and hands it back.

Thank you.

Colette takes the tube and places it into a professional-looking box.

I love the show, by the way. Would it be all right – if – could we get a picture?

Colette smiles and gets her phone out. She's all flustered. Annie intervenes smoothly.

Annie Let's do the selfie later, shall we, Colette?
OK, everyone, that's lovely. I'm gonna ask you to just sum up for the viewers now, Jack. And: action.

Jack (*deadpan*) Well, folks, I just gobbed in a tube and now I can't wait to see what happens.

4. JACK'S DRESSING ROOM

A star's changing room: Eames-type chair and footrest, table with lights. Jack (in a Simpsons *dressing gown) sits, eyes closed and cross-legged, on his daybed. Dane taps on the door and enters immediately.*

Dane What up, Jack? What you doin'?

Jack Meditating. How was that?

Dane We just shot that canteen scene. That guy wouldn't know how to frame a shot if he'd been injected with liquid Spielberg.

Jack gets up, takes off his dressing gown, under which he wears his on-set outfit.

Jack He got everything he needed to complete the scene though, right?

Dane He always gets what he needs. (*bored Brit voice*) 'Establishing wide shot. Move in for the mid. Two singles. Inserts.' And then: 'Lunch!'
My right nipple could direct better than this guy.
I tell ya, there ain't enough Black and brown talent on this show.
Nearly everybody's a white guy with tattoos. Even the woman who plays your mom. Can't you do something?

Jack You do something, they're your people.

Dane That's how you do me? Shiiiiiiiiiiiiit.
'They're *your* people' – what am I, Moses?? (*inhales and exhales*) Say, how's . . . (*announcer voice*) CELEBRITY D-N-A!

Jack Filming finished a while back. They've called my agent, I don't know what about.

Dane They probably watched every episode of season one and now know just what a terrible actor you are.

Jack I'd probably have reached the top by now if I didn't have you clinging to my shirt tails.

Dane I think my relentless starlight shines on you, making you far more attractive than you actually are.

Jack gives up, puts his surgeon's mask on, laughs.

Jack You wanna run the scene?

5. OPERATING-ROOM SET

Jack and Dane change into costume and stroll onto the set as the scenery changes behind them.
 It's a tense operation scene. There are others on the OR team, but we focus on Jack and Dane as their characters Dr Zach and Dr Jaheim operate. Jaheim questions Zach's every move.

Zach Please may I have more suction here? Soon as possible – thank you . . .

Jaheim Do people really say that in this situation?

Zach They do if they want to stop the patient bleeding to death.

Jaheim Just trying to lighten the –

A huge gout of blood spurts from the person on the operating table.

Zach This is bad. Bad, bad, bad, bad, bad, bad! FUCK!

Jaheim Dude's bleedin' like a crack dealer in an alleyway. (*yells*) We need more blood up in here! And I mean now! MORE BLOOD!

Zach's trying to staunch the bleeding. It's hard work.

People run back and forth, attaching blood bags to stands near the patient.

Zach (*focused*) Stop yelling. THEY KNOW WHAT TO DO!!

Jaheim Says you.

A long, unending beep from the nearby monitor.
Jaheim grabs the defibrillator.

Defib!

Zach CHARGE TO FIFTEEN. CLEAR!

And they go to work — several times — but the monitor's endless beep continues and then stops.
They take a pulse. Look at each other. No sign of life.
Zach is destroyed — Jaheim next to him. They lost a patient. It's horrible.
Jaheim supportively puts a hand on Zach's shoulder

Jaheim (*in solidarity*) Maybe let me finish up next time?

Zach You know what? Fuck you, Jaheim. He might still be alive if you weren't screwing around. It's not *Showtime at the Apollo* in here. This is our job! We're trying to save someone's life. You should fuckin' know better!

Jaheim glares at Zach — then exits.

Winn And cut!

Everyone takes a moment — Dane re-enters and hugs Jack. It was a good scene. The show's flamboyant British director, Winn Grant, (white, fifties), makes a quick announcement. Annie watches from nearby.

Winn We'll do mid shots and close-ups next, so be back in a few minutes and we'll readjust the lighting while you're splashing your loafers.

If Documentary Queen wants to shoot a little B-roll here, she should go ahead.

Annie's very excited. Her crew are rolling and we see Jack and co. on screen.

Annie We've got your results!

Dane reacts immediately to this news:

Dane I hate when people say that.
 Jack, don't admit to a *damn* thing. This kid might not be yours. If you cop to this, you'll be paying college fees till you're dead.

Jack (*teasing*) Dane, do you mind? I have documentary things to attend to with *this* camera crew. In *this* area. You need to piss off back to your *own* area . . .

Dane looks at Jack, raises an imaginary handbag.

Dane (*very camp*) Please yourself: I'm all about the glamour, baby. (*giving it Whitney Houston*) And I – EE I EE I EE I – will alwaaaaays luuurve you . . .

And swishes away: a drag queen in scrubs.

Jack (*laughs*) That was funny – right? You should keep that in.

Annie *Anything* funny we keep in, don't worry. In fact, I might get him to do it all again if he can remember what he did.

Jack You'd shoot that again? What about spontaneity?

Annie Spontaneity? Listen, I dated a cameraman; he shot all the seventies David Attenborough documentaries. You think those flying squirrels just take off when the guy says 'Action'? They had trainees up trees for hours throwing those things one after the other to get the money shot. Attenborough never knew; he just kept saying: (*does Attenborough to a tee*) 'This . . . is the magic of wildlife.'

Jack (*laughs*) I don't care; I love that guy.

Annie So . . . Jack, you might want to sit down for this bit.

A moment of gravitas here as Annie positions herself to deliver the news. Jack sits on the operating table.

You met Dr Colette Murchison last time, but you weren't properly introduced. You remember – she's from the Columbia University DNA Research Department.

THE BIG PAYBACK: THE PLAY

Colette appears and shakes hands with Jack. She sits and is still a bit starstruck. She shakes it off and begins.

Colette Sorry about last time. Your selfie's on my mum's bedside table now. So, thank you.

Annie clears her throat.

So. We've spent a considerable amount of time calibrating your test results. As always on *Celebrity DNA*, we seek to pinpoint your forefathers so accurately there'll be no doubting who they were or what they got up to in the past.

Jack Sounds intriguing. Can't wait . . .

She picks up a large envelope with a flourish.

Colette I have the results here.

She spreads out the paperwork. A large family tree appears on the screen (like a sci-fi version of Pete Frame's Rock Family Trees).
Camera shifts round to Colette as she traces the timeline with her finger.

(*clears throat*) Well, as you say, your parents, Ramsay and Morag Braddock, reside in Loch Fyne.

Jack intervenes. As she shows him pictures of his mum and dad and their lovely house, which is in landscaped grounds in Loch Fyne.

Jack Yeah, that's right. I was very fortunate to spend my childhood up there. I spent most of my time riding horses and fishing with my dad. But in the end, I wanted more, and I went to look for it in good old London.

Colette Yes, but this show isn't about you, it's about your forefathers. Tracing the timeline from your parents, we now know that your grandfather was John and that his father was William and that his father was Hugh. But if we jump back to Jamaica in 1751 . . .

Jack Whoa, whoa, whoa! Jamaica? Why are we jumping back to Jamaica? I'm Scottish.

Colette (*interrupting*) Actually, 30 per cent of the plantations in Jamaica were owned by Scots; your ancestors played a large role in that activity. So if we look here, we find your forefathers, Lachlan Braddock and his wife Elsbeth – they ran Braddock's plantation in the Clarendon district of Jamaica. This was a few miles from Pindar's Valley, their immediate rivals.

Jack has turned white. Dane has wandered back, entranced by what he's hearing. Jack turns to look at him, then back at Colette, who continues.

We've found many examples of how the plantation was run, which makes for . . . well, you'll hear . . .

She hands him a piece of paper – the text appears on the screen. Jack voices over:

Jack Braddock regularly punished slaves with ferocious floggings and other brutish and vile chastisements. In 1756, a runaway slave called Pharaoh was recaptured. Braddock had both of his feet put in shackles; gagged him; cuffed his hands; rubbed him with molasses; and left him naked all night to be assailed by flies and mosquitoes.

Dane moves towards him to support but Jack raises his hand like: 'Not now.' He raises his voice at Annie.

I'm sorry but this feels like a fucken ambush! I don't know anything about this. My mum and dad have never said – they would've told me – I had no idea . . .

He looks at Dane.

Dane Why you lookin' at me? You volunteered to be on this dumbass show in the first place.

Jack Dane, I'm so sorry.

Colette Mr Braddock, if you'll allow me to continue. I have some excerpts from the Braddock journal. Turns out the master of the estate was quite prolific. According to this, he wrote a daily journal concerning all his activities on the estate.

She takes a second piece of parchment and begins to read.
   Fade to black.
   On screen: we see the words as we hear Colette read. It's a short paragraph from a slave owner's diary jottings.

THE BIG PAYBACK: THE PLAY

(*voice-over*) 'On reaching the estate, I was informed that six Negroes were to be punished. The first was a man of about thirty-five years of age, a cattle herder. His offence was having allowed a mule to go astray. At the command of the overseer, he proceeded to strip off part of his clothes and laid himself flat on his belly, his back and buttocks being uncovered. One of the drivers then began flogging him with the cart whip . . . causing the blood to spring at every stroke. When I saw the degraded and mangled victim writhing and groaning, I felt horror-struck. I trembled and felt sick.'

Blackout.

6. THE BRADDOCKS' LIVING ROOM

Delyse sits with Amelia and does her hair. Amelia is very upset and fragile about being fired.

Delyse People get fired all the time.

Amelia Mum, don't.

Delyse No – they do. When your grandma was a nurse, she got fired from her job five times – every time they give her the job back the next week.

Amelia How come?

Delyse She'd go back and the people on security would just let her back in – she'd be in uniform; nobody took a blind bit of notice that this Black girl in nurse's uniform was on the ward. She said: 'I'd be there three days and nobody would say a blasted thing! Then Sister take me to one side and say "How come you're back? We sacked you."' And she'd say: 'Nobody stop me coming back here – we all look the bloody same to you.'

Amelia That's not true.

Delyse It is.

Amelia Well I'm the only Afro-Caribbean teacher at this school – everyone knows who I am.

Delyse You're notorious.

Amelia But I don't want to be, I just want to teach. (*starts crying again*)

Shelton enters. He's wearing overalls, eating a pattie and tool kit.

Shelton What's she bawling about now?

Delyse You know, it wouldn't hurt you to show some sympathy once in a while.

Shelton All I said was what she bawling about?

Amelia I lost my job, Dad!

Delyse You never lost your job, darling, you give it away.

Amelia Mum!

Shelton It's true – you get yourself involved in stupidness. They find out and they sack you backside. I woulda done the same. I'm goin' through things too, y'know? Nobody even gives me a second thought.

Delyse (*mocking*) Ahhh, you want me to run a bath for you?

Shelton That would be nice.

Delyse Run your own bath, you unsympathetic, bad-minded wretch. Seven days she been out of work and all we're hearing from you is jokes. You don't have no heart?

Shelton Of course I've got a heart. But I need money. If Amelia's got money stashed away to invest in my business, then we can talk. If we ain't got that – we might lose the house.

Delyse You serious?

Shelton Like a heart attack.

Delyse Lord Jesus Christ.

Amelia What are you going to do?

Glenroy enters on crutches – flops down on the couch.

Glenroy Evening – not good news.

Delyse What the doctor say?

Glenroy Says the repair's gonna take some time. It's the ACL, I got a big-ass tear on my cruciate ligament. Doc says it's gonna need surgery. Could be an eighteen-week wait. If they get it wrong, I could never walk again. I might as well chop off my foot now.

Delyse God, are you serious?

Glenroy It's the most serious thing you can imagine.

Shelton That's more serious than me not getting a bank loan?

Delyse This is the boy's career, it's not just about buying more vehicles for a delivery service.

Shelton That's my career!

Delyse No, it's not, that's the business you'd like to be in – you have one car, you'd like two more with drivers to match.

Shelton Why you repeating my scenario like that? Has this been on the news?

Delyse I'm saying the boy's career was wrapped up in sports from the time he was a baby. Now they telling him he'll never play basketball again.

Shelton There's money in darts.

Delyse What did I tell you about these flippant remarks? One more and I'll chop off yu tings with a breadknife.

Shelton Look, everybody, it's my job to go out in the world and protect my family.

Delyse What? You gonna wave yu magic wand? You're the Jamaican Dumbledore? If you were, we'd be living in a castle.

Glenroy They'd never have a Black Dumbledore. He'd never fit the pointy hat on his afro.

Amelia Why are you all talking about Harry Potter? What am I gonna do about my job?

Delyse Sweetie, listen – if you really want that job, then you're going to have to lawyer up: y'need money for that. You think you've been unfairly dismissed?

Amelia Yes – that's exactly what I think.

Delyse Well, then we have to fight back. And if they don't back down, next time we see them, I'll bring me bread knife.

7. ANTHONY WEBBER'S OFFICE

Jack sits waiting in the Webber Entertainment Agency. There's a logo and perhaps a mixtape sizzle reel of TV and movie stars smiling at the camera. Cheesy but cool.
 Anthony enters and fixes Jack with a sympathetic stare.

Anthony I heard about *Celebrity DNA*-gate. The shit really hit the fan, huh?

Jack Why didn't my mum and dad they tell me where the family money came from? This is a fucken nightmare!

Anthony (*exhales*) Jack, Jack, Jack. Nearly everyone in this town has blood relations who did something a smidge shitty back in the day. Whether it's Nazis or the KGB or the Romans or the transatlantic slave trade.

Jack has his head in his hands as he listens. He moans.

Jack You can't allow this show to be broadcast. It'll kill my career.

Anthony crosses over to him, kneels, looks into his eyes.

Anthony Kill your career? Are you kidding? Nobody's gonna say a goddamn thing about you, and if they do, we'll litigate so fast, they'll think they've been bitch-slapped by Fresh Prince. OK, big deal – your forefathers were plantation owners. So what? It's just the way the world is. You shake anybody's family tree, there's gonna be a shower of shit at some point.

Jack (*rocking/moaning*) I don't want to be showered in shit. I've done Shakespeare in Regent's Park. I've got two Best Actor Emmys. Not one whiff of scandal.

Anthony Jack. Annie Clayton is a respected director for a major network. She won't give up on this programme easily. It's her only income – not only that, she tells me the footage they've cut so far is dynamite.

THE BIG PAYBACK: THE PLAY

Jack Can't you just make this go away?

Anthony You signed a binding contract. Besides, you run away from this now, you'll look like a heartless son of a bitch who doesn't care about Black people, slavery and the whole nine yards. My advice? Lean all the way into it. Do some research. At least look like you care. You'll come out smelling of roses.

Jack OK. That makes sense. I'll do some reading. I wanna at least look like a decent human being.

He gets up and heads out the door.
Anthony releases a long breath.

8. JACK'S APARTMENT

Jack sits on an Eames chair, a table next to him. He drinks whisky, whilst highlighting passages in a book – one of many piled up next to him.
The door buzzer goes. Jack picks up the entryphone, looks and sees Dane looking back. He buzzes him in. Jack returns his chair. Dane enters. He's got beers and Chinese food.

Dane The hero returns. . . I . . . uh . . . over-ordered. I got overwhelmed at the digital menu. It was beautifully photographed. Like a dim sum catwalk show. Anyway – it smells delicious. (*puts stuff down*) How's the research?

Jack Listen. (*reads*) 'When slavery was abolished, they gave the slave owners, the plantation bosses 20 million pounds in compensation for their lost property.' Do you know how much that is in today's money?? Seventeen billion quid. The freed slaves got nothing. How could they let this happen?

Dane I thought you said your manager told you to do this for the PR. You sound like you actually care now.

Jack I do care.

Dane I would never go on this programme in a million years. You know why? Cos white folks go on and find out they related to a king or queen. Our stories are different. You scratch any one of us and you find the word SLAVE; we don't need to be reminded of it all the time.

Just cos your forefathers were slavers, that don't mean you gotta (*announcer voice*) 'Save the Entire Black Population of the World'. You're just you, remember?

Jack But isn't it my responsibility to do something? Shouldn't I make some kind of reparation? They've been trying to make an argument about this for years. People haven't been treated right.

Dane What about affirmative action? There's been a Black president. We've got Black and brown movie stars and directors. We got gays in the military. One day? I'm gonna direct a Netflix show and surprise the shit out of everybody. But I can only do that because someone did it before me.

Sidney Poitier struggled before me, Oscar Micheaux did it before him; we stand on everybody's shoulders and we here. You can't support the weight of your forefathers alone. That shit'll fuck up your knees.

Jack shakes his head and starts opening Chinese food containers.

Jack Wanna get some plates and some cutlery?

Dane just stares at him.

Dane (*badass*) Motherfucker, do I look like I work for you? I went and *got* this shit. *You* get the goddamn plates and cutlery.

Jack laughs despite himself.

I know, I know. Too soon?

9. SOHO EDITING SUITE

On screen: shots of media-tastic Soho. Then a logo for an edit suite: 'SohoCutz.com'.

Annie greets Jack with a big hug. Jack just stands there refusing to return the embrace. Annie, realising the hug isn't taking, releases him.

Annie So . . . How was your flight?

Jack It was OK. I'm nearly at the end of the Fast & Furious movie franchise.

Annie Do you want coffee?

Jack Why don't we just get to it?

Annie Look, I know you have strong feelings about the show, but you come out of it really well.

Jack (*hard to say*) I don't wanna (*mimics her*) 'come out of it really well'. Sounds like I'm getting away with something when you say that.

I feel like I've got to do something to make up for this. Some kind of reparation. It's all I've been thinking about. There's gotta be something I can do.

Annie I've seen this kind of thing before. People feel guilty for something terrible that happened centuries ago. Think they've got to fix it. It's not your job. You don't have to fix anything.

Jack If it's not my job, then what am I doing here? You can't stir up all these feelings and just expect me to . . . cooperate in your nice little life-ruining fuckin' television programme. I haven't slept since I found out.

She looks at him and wills him to calm down. Miraculously, he does so. She inhales. Uses her horse-whisperer voice.

Annie So the good news is that there are some options here. I've got money left in the budget for a trip to Jamaica. We could film you in situ on location. Walking in the footsteps of your ancestors.

Jack (*breaks*) NO Fuckin' Way. Just poke my eyes out with a sharp stick now. NO!

Annie Hang on, I haven't told you –

Jack I'm not gonna stand in a field where my ancestors made a ton o' money from slaves and pretend it's just a cute little documentary. I'm not doing that.

Annie inhales, then breathes out. Makes a decision.

Annie Well, that's good because that saves the production money.

Jack I don't give a flyin' f—

Annie Your other option, of course, is we go to the Midlands and meet the descendants of your forefathers' slaves.

Jack The Midlands?

Annie Yeah. On your DNA tests, we got a massive hit in the Midlands. There was one in Baltimore, a couple in Brooklyn, but an entire family in the Midlands. They're called the Braddocks. They're a Black working-class family.

Jack holds his stomach, takes a deep breath.

Jack I'm related to Black people? How come I look like this? That doesn't make sense.

Annie (*carefully*) It doesn't quite work that way – they're related to you because of what your forefathers did to the slave women.

It dawns on Jack.
OH FUCK.
Annie continues regardless.

They live somewhere called Acocks Green. The dad, Shelton, drives a white van, the mum's called Delyse and runs a food bank. The daughter, Amelia, is a teacher, and the son, Glenroy, is an athlete. They're willing to meet you, Jack. I think you'll like them.

Jack (*thinks*) And they're part of my bloodline?

Annie That's one way of putting it.

Jack reacts to that . . .

10. VAN

Jack and Annie use chairs to assemble the interior of a Ford Transit – with Jack riding shotgun as Annie drives; the crew (sound dude: white, thirties; camera guy: Black, thirties) sleep in the back.
We hear driving noises.
Jack's ringtone blares ('I'm Gonna Be (500 Miles)' by The Proclaimers). He picks up a tablet and flicks it on.
Dane's face fills the big screen.

Dane What up, buddy?

Jack is troubled. He exhales. Shakes his head.

Jack Hey.

THE BIG PAYBACK: THE PLAY

Dane notices Jack's reluctance.

Dane Come on, Jack. You're doing a good thing. I'm proud of you, man.

Jack I just don't want 'em to hate me.

Dane You're gonna be fine. I wish I could be there with you . . . particularly for the moment when they tie you up and shove you in the basement.

Jack (*ignores him*) I need to work out what I'm gonna say when I get there.

Dane My advice? Just listen. I love you, man.

Jack I love you too. I appreciate it. Speak to you when I get to the other side.

He presses his iPad to hang up. Annie smiles.

Annie He's got your back, right?

Jack I think so. I really hope so. I mean – this is a massive test for our friendship. He's just found out that his best friend's ancestors owned a plantation.
If I was him, I think I'd want to put distance between us.

Annie You don't want that. You're a loyal friend. That's not who you are.

Jack Sometimes I have no idea who I am. All I know is I want to do right by anyone who's been tainted by this.

Annie Jack, you are not personally responsible for the actions of your forefathers.

Jack (*yells*) I wish everybody'd stop saying that. Somebody's got to take responsibility.

He goes quiet, reaches forward, turns on the radio. Quiet music plays. He stares out the window.
A sign on the screen gives a number of views of Acocks Green, Birmingham, UK. Lovely . . .

11. THE BRADDOCKS' FAMILY HOME

Annie and the sound and camera dudes wait as Jack works up the courage to knock.

Annie OK. Well, I think you're ready. We've been standing out here a while. You feel briefed about what we have to do, right?

Jack Colette filled me in. The genealogy guy you put me in touch with was great. I've got my DNA map. And breath mints. Pepper spray . . . Tasers . . .

They laugh. Although Jack looks as serious as a heart attack.

Annie What do you think their reaction's going to be?

Jack I don't know. I just want to know how I can make it up to them.

Annie You just have to present your case . . . and then listen. Keep saying to yourself: 'It's not my job to fix anything. I'm just here to show some empathy.'

Jack I know, I know. Let's go.

But he doesn't ring the doorbell – just stands and waits.

12. THE BRADDOCKS' FAMILY HOME

Inside the Braddocks' abode, there's bustling activity – a dining table has been laid nicely. Shelton enters, carrying the largest bowl of soup you've ever seen.

Amelia follows, also carrying a bowl, but it's smaller. She places hers on the table and resumes arguing as if it's been going on all afternoon.

Amelia Why'd he have to come here? Why couldn't we meet somewhere neutral? Like the community centre? Or down a dark alleyway?

Shelton He's coming to talk about his ancestors, and how they used to own our ancestors. He must feel guilty.

Amelia He should – I've been reading about his family and what they got up to.

Shelton Yes, but it's not him, is it? He's just that guy off the telly you used to fancy.

Amelia I never fancied him.

Glenroy enters as she says this.

Glenroy Every time he was on, you'd lick the screen.

Amelia That happened once, I was drunk, and you weren't even here.

Glenroy carries his soup bowl with aplomb – places it down and sits. He inhales the soup and sighs.

Glenroy (*loving it*) This is big big food, man. Hard food mek a man strong. Innit? When I finish this? You could just stick me *and* Jude Bellingham on 'gainst *Germany* and we'd kick them backside.

Shelton Wid your bruk-up foot? How you goin' manage that?

Delyse enters, checking her watch – vexed.

Delyse Why can't white people tell time? Now we to have to wait till he gets here.

Shelton Wait for what? I've been working like Kunta Kinte all day and I'm hungry! Put my man's food in the oven and let the rest of us eat.

Amelia I agree with Dad. All I've been doing is studying online and I could eat something. White people ain't got no manners.

Glenroy I've had two dumplings while you've been chatting foolishness.

Delyse Put one more piece of food in yu mouth before I've said grace and you're sleeping outside tonight. We don't eat till Jack gets here. He's family now.

Amelia Jesus, Mum. His ancestors raped our ancestors.

Delyse Don't use language like that. That is not his fault. He wants to meet. I say he eats with us; we're decent people.

The doorbell rings.

Shelton He's here.

Delyse We just have to act natural.

Amelia You do you and I'll do me.

Delyse has gone for a moment – they all wait – Glenroy tries to scoop some yam into his spoon, but Amelia stops him.
  Lighting changes, and the screen shows shots of the room and the family as the camera enters and films Jack's entrance. The following is enhanced by cutaways on the screen.
  Annie briefs everyone before they begin shooting for real.

Annie (*quietly*) OK, everyone. Thank you so much for allowing us to be here. Just behave as though the camera isn't here. This'll be an extended take – the finale of *Celebrity DNA: Jack Braddock*. We'll roll camera now. You won't even know we're here.

She steps away behind the camera.

(*loud*) Sync clap, *Jack Braddock Celeb DNA* take one!

She claps in front of the boom mic.
  Delyse enters with an even bigger bowl of soup with hard food.

Delyse Mr Braddock.

Jack Call me Jack.

Amelia Yeah, cos we're family now.

Glenroy Him and us are family.

Amelia That's right, Glenroy.

Glenroy Rah. Can you lend me, like, twenty grand?

Amelia He shouldn't lend – he should just give it you.

Delyse (*stern*) Amelia.

Jack fumbles, hanging his jacket off the chair. He struggles to say something important.

Jack I've never been – I mean to say – I mean, this is my first – so – to be clear – I've been to Dane's place – but I work with him – you know? I mean this really is –

Amelia You're saying the only Black household you've ever been in is your friend Dane's house from the TV show? Your Black co-star.

THE BIG PAYBACK: THE PLAY

Jack I guess I am saying that.

Amelia looks at everyone askance.

Amelia How's this gonna work?

Shelton Let the man sit down and eat his food. He's just come all the way from London – I bet he's starvin'.

Jack I could eat something.

He sits at the table and studies his bowl of food.

Wow. This smells great. What is it?

Delyse It's Saturday soup. With mutton and hard food. You want a pint of water wid it?

Jack looks at the food some more – it does smell good.

Jack Well, I . . .

Shelton / Glenroy / Amelia You'll want water with it.

Delyse pours out water for Jack. Everyone sits. Jack's about to eat but Delyse touches his arm. She wants to say grace.

Delyse (*earnest*) Heavenly Father, bless this food, for which we have toiled throughout this winter's day. Lord bless this man, this two-time Emmy winner, Jack Braddock.
And surely, bound to win again this year for his amazin' performance as Dr Zach in *Forensic MDs*.

Shelton Delyse? You doin' his entire CV? Hurry up nuh? Is hungry mi hungry?

Delyse (*ignoring*) Lord, this young man has come to Birmingham to discover his relatives and this is us! We are his blood, and we gather here today, to eat this carefully prepared and delicious meal of Saturday soup with mutton and hard food and one and two potato.

Amelia This is just too weird.

Shelton Amelia, quiet; yu mother preaching. She soon get the spirit.

Delyse When this young man find out about us, he could have easily run a mile, Lord. To distance himself from this relationship.

This un-fort-u-nate relationship that has been exhumed by scientists and historians and whatnot – and filmed by Annie – God bless her – for people to watch on the television or phone or tablet.

Amelia Christ Almighty.

Delyse shoots her a look, but continues regardless.

Delyse But Jack never did distance himself. So I say unto him – and the rest of the crew – welcome to our house, here in Acocks Green, Birmingham. Let us now eat and welcome him.

Glenroy lifts his spoon and then pauses. Delyse nods and they all chow down.

Shelton Delyse likes a long prayer – anything shorter than one side of a LP and she kick up a fuss.

Glenroy What's an LP?

Shelton You heathen.

Amelia How's the soup, Mr Braddock?

She says this as Jack turns bright red and takes a rather large gulp from his pint glass of water.

Jack It's delicious. Hot. Very hot.

He takes another gulp from the glass, draining the lot.

Shelton The soup hot, yes? Mind it don't incinerate y'backside.

Amelia pours him some more water. He drinks half a pint, but keeps eating. Shelton nods approvingly.

Amelia So. Jack. You've come to see how the other half lives.

Jack Well, obviously I wanted to meet you – after I found out that we're – you know – related by blood.

Shelton So, Mr Braddock, you on some kind of cultural safari?

Jack Absolutely not. I wanted to meet you and say . . .

Amelia Here it comes.

Delyse Let him talk, Amelia –

Jack I wanted to meet you and look you in the eye and ask if there's anything I can do to make your lives better.

Shelton, Delyse and Glenroy stare at him. Annie nudges her cameraman to get close-ups of each face – concerned, amused, angry, empathic.

Shelton What is goin' on in your head, Mr Braddock?

Jack It's Jack.

Shelton 'Anything you could do to make my life better'? You could go back in time and shoot your ancestors.

A mini-beat.

Jack I can't say I blame you for saying that. I've read how they treated the slaves on that plantation. It was a disgrace.

Amelia So, I assume you've come here to say 'sorry'.

Jack glances at the camera, straight on the lens – he's confused – the next few exchanges overlap . . .

Jack I wasn't really thinking about apologising; it was more about what I could do to make things better.

Amelia So you can feel less guilty?

Jack Hang on.

Amelia Without actually saying sorry?

Jack I didn't personally do anything, so –

Amelia So what're you doing here then?

Jack I just feel I owe you something, but I'm not here to apologise. It wasn't me who enslaved your ancestors.

Amelia Oh come on, I've looked you up. You grew up in a castle, went to private school – you've benefited from all that inherited, unearned, undeserved wealth. I say we hold him down and set fire to his feet.

Delyse We not doing that in the house.

Glenroy Any foot fire's gotta be outside. This carpet's new.

Shelton All right, stop the noise.

Jack, you see us? We're a strong family. I drive a delivery van. I've had it six years. When it bruk down, it's me who fix it. If I can't fix, I can't work.

I apply to the bank for a loan to buy a couple more vans – so I could create more jobs and provide work for friends and family.

The bank say I don't possess the financial infrastructure to take on some ting like that – my own business. I bet someone like you wouldn't have a problem getting a loan like that.

I even had a good name for my business – 'Mi Soon Come. Deliveries at the touch of a button. Call 0800 788 6599.'

Amelia Point is, Jack's family got their pay-off after slavery – we're still waiting for our forty acres and a mule. And they can't even give Dad a loan for another van. It's always been a rigged deck in this country – and it's fucked.

Everyone looks at Delyse.

Delyse Amelia! What have I told you about using that language in this house? Mr Braddock's come a long way – show him some respect? You want any ting else to eat, Mr Braddock?

Jack It's just Jack.

Shelton I never got my bank loan. I'm still driving my knackered old van, doing deliveries all day, every day – I work Sundays sometimes – it's hard.

Jack It sounds it. (*he ponders*) I have to say, I've been very lucky.

Amelia That's one word for it. They're gonna pay you a million per episode for next season.

Glenroy If I had money like that, I wouldn't even live on Earth, man. I'd live on Jupiter or sutten.

Amelia Glenroy, if you lived on Jupiter how would you watch *Match of the Day* and Netflix and all that?

Glenroy I'd have satellite – it'd be nearer up there, wouldn't it?

Amelia Not only are you getting paid serious cheddar from next year on, Mr Braddock, you've been earning that kind of cash since you started. You're well minted. So why are you here? Have you come

THE BIG PAYBACK: THE PLAY

to pay us off because you feel guilty? Or are you actually gonna do something constructive to help? And why hasn't he said sorry yet?

Jack is frazzled at this point. Where is this going?

Jack (*to Annie*) Look, maybe we should stop filming? This isn't going how I thought it was gonna go – I just need to get my bearings . . .

He's looking for Annie to help him out or cut, but she's rolling her hands as if to say, 'Keep going, it's great!'

(*with great difficulty*) Look. I'm not saying I don't come from, y'know, privilege, but I worked really hard to – you don't know what I've had to go through to get where I am.

The family look at him and then at each other disbelievingly, like: 'This fucking guy . . .'

(*digging himself deeper*) It hasn't been easy. I work twelve-hour days – sometimes I work weekends. I don't see my friends and my family – and now this has happened –

The family's reaction. Can this get any worse to raatid?

(*breaking down*) I know you don't mean to, but I feel like you're ganging up on me . . . I feel like I – like I deserve it . . . but I didn't do anything.

Annie I've cut cameras! You've done more than enough.

Amelia The weeping was a bit over the top – unless you were acting –

Jack collects himself – the women give him the space to do that. He tries to regain control.

Jack Amelia, I came here because I want to do the right thing. I wanna make reparation. Is there something I can do for you – some kind of compensation for –

Amelia For what? Slavery? For the fact your forefathers raped mine? That your family are still living off the benefits of that, for never paying us a penny, for all the work that we did to put money in your pockets? That's . . . very nice of you to ask what you can do for me . . . But I don't want your charity. My problems are mine and my family's and we don't need you.

Delyse Amelia, just tell the man what happen. You too intense.

Amelia glares at Jack.

Amelia He doesn't wanna hear my crap. What? He's gonna fall to his knees and give us the loose change from his pockets? No, man, I've got more dignity than that.

Jack I'd be honoured to listen to your story.

She thinks about it – looks at Annie – who is poised – she nods and Annie's all over it like a rash.

Annie Turnover – and – action.

Amelia OK. You asked for it. I'm a teacher, English and History, Churchill Green Secondary Academy. Lot of kids of colour there. It's like the grime tent at Glastonbury most days. I love it, though. The students, contrary to all the tabloid bullshit you may have read, all want to learn.

Shelton You have standards –

Glenroy Impossibly high.

Amelia Hello? You've had your turn. So, yeah – I've been at this school a while and – then, the head teacher calls me in and asks me to run Black History Month – and at first, I'm vex? You know – why me?

Jack Because . . . you're –

Amelia I KNOW why!

But I didn't feel a way about it – cos it was gonna either be me – or Mr Simmit, the gym teacher. I got tights with a higher IQ than this guy; or Doris, one of the dinner ladies. So it had to be me, right? And I'm dil-li-gent, I've got all the age-appropriate books and videos and everything, and the first Black History Month is a blast. They come to me again – I run it again . . . boom!

Kids' awareness of Black issues and heritage goes up, like 40, 50, 60 per cent – they're making me proud . . . yeah, knowledge of their heritage made them begin to carry themselves in a different way than they used to . . . you know . . .

Glenroy She's not the only one with a sad story? I was a baller at

THE BIG PAYBACK: THE PLAY

school. I was NBA all the way. But none of that lottery money goes to basketball in the UK. You know why? Cos we don't medal in the tournaments. All that sponsorship money goes to the posh-white-man sports – archery, rowing, fuckin' sailing! All that bullshit. Normal Black athletes are left high and dry.

Amelia The sports lottery is the largest transfer of money from poor people that directly helps to finance rich white people's pursuits.

Glenroy I wanted a scholarship to play basketball in the States, then I picked up an injury, wrecked my ACL – that's it. All over. But I know what you're sayin' – (*Scottish accent*) 'You could still coach, Glenroy.' Yeah? But check this, I've applied for sponsorship, funding – and it's non-existent. I'll never coach in this country. That's what happens if you choose a Black-man sport. I shoulda took up rowing. If I'd done that, injury or no injury I'd still have a career.

Now Glenroy's upset.

Jack That's terrible.

Amelia Can I finish my story please?

Omnes All right / You haffe shout? / Sorry sis.

Amelia (*takes a breath*) Post George Floyd, and Black Lives Matter, things changed. The kids wanted to know more about police brutality in the UK, Toxteth, Broadwater Farm; the States too: civil rights, Emmett Till, Malcom X . . . it was too much to fit into just one month.

So I organised Black History studies on Saturday mornings – for anyone interested in digging into their Black legacy. Thing is, though, I didn't tell the head teacher. There were complaints from a couple white parents that their kids were being 'excluded', that this was 'reverse racism', that I was 'inciting hatred', 'radicalising' . . .

Jack But you were just teaching, right?

Amelia (*upset*) They fired me. All the kids stood up for me. I appealed. They wouldn't take me back. I got branded as a troublemaker in the local papers. I can't teach any more. (*breaking*) But educating those kids, the ones who wanted to learn and know about who they are – that was something. If I had a mobile library I'd just drive round and do it for free.

Jack Look. You're all family to me now, right? I know what I've got to do. I want to make reparation.

There's a moment when the family, once again, just look at him. Is this what they want?

Shelton What, like a handout?

Jack NO. Proper reparation. Shelton – I can buy you two vans. New ones. Glenroy – I can sponsor a local basketball team, you'd coach, and we can create the best basketball team in the UK! Amelia –

Amelia's listening now.

You want a new, well-stocked mobile library? Consider it done.

Delyse Jack. That is so kind and generous. I've prayed and prayed that one day the answer to all our problems would be solved like this. If only more white people were like you . . .

Amelia's had enough.

Amelia (*yells*) MUM! HE'S NOT JESUS!
(*to Jack*) I DON'T WANT YOUR CHARITY. I'M NOT YOUR LITTLE SLAVE GIRL THAT YOU CAN JUST . . . JUST . . . PAY OFF!

Jack No, you're not. I don't think of you as a 'little slave girl'. I don't even see race –

Amelia, in a rage, charges at Jack (surprising even herself) and knocks him over, straddles him and starts hitting him.

Amelia You don't. Get to. Come here. With your fuckin' blood money!
And buy us off! Like we're! Fuckin' stupid! D'you hear me? I AM, NOT YOUR. FUCKIN' VICTIM! I SAID DO YOU HEAR ME!

Jack YES! I HEAR YOU. AND I'M SORRY! I'M REALLY SORRY. I'M SO SORRY.

Jack is curled up in a bundle saying 'Sorry.' Amelia's exhausted. Frustrated. Embarrassed.
Tears are running down Jack's face.

They're all staring at him, blank-faced . . . disbelieving.

Amelia Now the apology. I think that's what therapists call a breakthrough.

Delyse, Glenroy and Shelton watch Jack weep.
Now, a kind of miraculous occurrence – Delyse, Amelia, Glenroy and Shelton all approach him and put a hand on a shoulder or his back, or his head. They stand there and comfort him in this, his moment of need. No words required.
Annie steps forward and waves her hands.

Annie And we cut. I think we've got what we need? Thank you so much, everyone – that was cathartic, no? We aired our grievances. There was a sincere apology. We had tears and even a smidgeon of ultra-violence. I think we got somewhere. Well done, everyone.

The Braddock family look at Jack. Then look at Annie. Then look at us.

13. FORENSIC MDS SET

On screen: it's a shooting day. Crew are bustling and hustling. We should notice that there are more Black and brown people, more women . . . it's not a big deal but it's noticeable. Jack's reading his script. He sees Dane approaching.

Jack Who wrote this shit?

Dane ambles up.

Dane Don't fuck with me, Jack! This took me weeks to write this episode. WEEKS!

Jack Did you spellcheck this? Oesophagus is not spelt with two 'e's at the beginning.

Dane That's a joke. It's a 'Let's take the piss out of Jack' typo. And, by the way, you need to remember: I'm not just your supporting actor today – I'm your boss.

Jack I hear you. Come on, let's get on with it.

Dane Hello, everyone, this is day one, block one of season three of *Forensic MDs*.

I'm your director today! First positions please.

Jack Directing suits you.

Dane Don't expect me to be grateful. You pleading my case to the network was the least you can do. But thanks anyway. That's what I call real reparations.

Jack Amen to that. Hey, did Annie get in touch with you about *Celebrity DNA*?

Dane I told her I wasn't doin' that shit – then she kinda Jedi mind-warped me . . .

On screen: the scene fades out, then in. Dane appears at a long table piled high with books; there are bookshelves behind.
A caption at the bottom of the screen reads:

'DANE BROWN – ACTOR: *FORENSIC MDS*'

We hear Annie Clayton's voice as Dane enters a book-lined room – it smells of privilege and exalted education.

Annie (*voice-over*) Dane has come to Westminster Abbey to meet Duncan Logan, a herald from the College of Arms and an expert in the pedigree of the most ancient families in the United Kingdom.

Dane sits at a table and is joined by Duncan, a young and studious-looking man. Duncan has paperwork with him; he places it in front of Dane.

Duncan Hi Dane, nice to meet you.

Dane Mr Logan – like Wolverine. SNIKT!

He holds his fists up à la Hugh Jackman. Duncan has no clue what he's on about.

Dane Great name . . .

Duncan I'm sure it is. Shall we sit?

Dane Sure, man, let's siddown and do this.

THE BIG PAYBACK: THE PLAY

Duncan So, you've been learning about your connections to Germany –

Dane Yeah – I'm like a cousin or great-great-infinity-grandson of Claude de Vergy. He was all up in the Portuguese aristocracy. Don't mean I get no pay cheque, though, right?

Duncan Well, you never know. We've done some homework on your behalf, and I want to show you your family tree, which we've just acquired. It shows your direct connection to these ancestors of yours.

> *We see over Dane's shoulder – we're looking at a family tree with a lot of names and lines through them . . .*

Dane Jesus, these are all, like, Germanic names? I'm German now? (*reads*) 'Elizabeth Albertina – Herzogin von Sachsen – Hildburghausen.' Well, I'm glad my great-great-grandma changed my name.

Duncan And if you'll look at the main ancestor in the red rectangle over your shoulder, we see a red rectangle at the bottom of the scroll. It says: Charlotte von Mecklenburg-Strelitz, Queen Consort of the United Kingdom, 1744–1818 . . . wife of George the Third . . .

Dane What's this mean?

Duncan It means you are directly related to Queen Charlotte, wife of King George the Third.

Dane Are you fuckin' kiddin' me?

Duncan Would you like a glass of water?

> *Dane is in shock.*
> *Snap to black.*
> *Ends.*

ACKNOWLEDGEMENTS

For a book ostensibly about compensation and repair for something that, for many people, ended two hundred years ago, it has been incredibly difficult to keep up with the new developments that keep on happening every day.

As we put the finishing touches to the manuscript for this book, the theme of the 38th African Union Summit held in Addis Ababa, Ethiopia, is 'Justice for Africans and People of African Descent Through Reparations'.

The first draft had to be updated even before the editors at Faber had finished reading it as the British prime minister, Keir Starmer, made fresh statements about the UK's position on reparations.

Trying to cover such a complex and constantly evolving subject has not been easy – we are not sure we would have taken it on had we realised how difficult it was going to be. We were only able to complete it due to the help and support of some really special people.

First of all, we would like to thank all the people we interviewed and featured in the book.

Thank you to Kehinde Andrews and Esther Stanford-Xosei, who were invaluable in shaping how we approached the subject.

Our endless gratitude to Robert Beckford, who gave his time and wisdom so freely and with such good cheer.

We are beyond grateful to Kenneth Mohammed, who we met through our research and who showed us how we can and should continue smiling, and even laughing, when tackling such painful and difficult subjects.

It was an absolute privilege to be able to tap into the massive brain that belongs to Bhavik Doshi, who gave us the confidence to explore reparations as a concrete reality as opposed to just a thought experiment.

We are always appreciative of any politician who puts their head above the parapet and is willing to go on the record around such a potentially contentious issue – thank you, Bell Ribeiro-Addy, MP.

A huge thanks to the editors at Faber, in particular Walter Donohue and Mikaela Pedlow, who helped shape many of our ramblings and bad grammar into a concise, sharp and readable book.

The book is only possible due to the intellectual work of so many who have written and researched this issue before us and so we are eternally thankful to them. While there are too many to name individually we would like to single out Sir Hilary Beckles, who is a giant in this field and stands head and shoulders above everyone else.

And finally, a massive thank-you must go to Hannah Ryder, in many ways the third writing partner, who has been a check and balance on so many of the ideas that Marcus brought to the table and who influenced the direction of the book in so many different ways.

FURTHER READING

Beckles, Hilary McDonald, *Britain's Black Debt: Reparations for Caribbean Slavery and Native Genocide* (University of West Indies Press, 2012)

Darity Jr, William A., and A. Kirsten Mullen, *From Here to Equality: Reparations for Black Americans in the Twenty-First Century* (University of North Carolina Press, 2020)

Ford, Clyde W., *Of Blood and Sweat: Black Lives and the Making of White Power and Wealth* (Amistad, 2022)

French, Howard W., *Born in Blackness: Africa, Africans, and the Making of the Modern World, 1471 to the Second World War* (Liveright, 2020)

Harding, Thomas, *White Debt: The Demerara Uprising and Britain's Legacy of Slavery* (Weidenfeld & Nicolson, 2022)

Hicks, Dan, *The Brutish Museums: The Benin Bronzes, Colonial Violence and Cultural Restitution* (Pluto Press, 2020)

Manjapra, Kris, *Black Ghost of Empire: The Long Death of Slavery and the Failure of Emancipation* (Penguin, 2023)

Neiman, Susan, *Learning from the Germans: Confronting Race and the Memory of Evil* (Penguin, 2020)

Rodney, Walter, *How Europe Underdeveloped Africa* (Verso, 2018)

Rosenthal, Caitlin, *Accounting for Slavery: Masters and Management* (Harvard University Press, 2018)

Táíwò, Olúfẹ́mi O., *Reconsidering Reparations: Why Climate Justice and Constructive Politics Are Needed in the Wake of Slavery and Colonialism* (Haymarket Books, 2025)

Thompson, Janna, *Should Current Generations Make Reparation for Slavery?* (Polity, 2018)

Williams, Eric, *Capitalism and Slavery* (Penguin Classics, 2022)

Winbush, Raymond A., *Should America Pay?: Slavery and the Raging Debate on Reparations* (Amistad, 2003)

NOTES

1: FLAGS, CHAINS AND TRUTH
1 Joe Flatman, 'Excavating the *CA* Archive: Black Country', *Current Archaeology*, 4 Feb. 2021.
2 Register of All-Party Parliamentary Groups, UK Parliament, 6 March 2024, publications.parliament.uk/pa/cm/cmallparty/240306/flags-and-heraldry.htm.
3 Poppy Brady, 'Fury Over Black Country "Slave Chains" Flag', *The Voice*, 10 July 2015.
4 Patrick Vernon, 'Black Country Flag Row: Why I Will Never Accept the Chain Logo', *Express & Star*, 14 July 2015.

2: BRITISH SLAVERY ENDED 1 FEBRUARY 2015
1 Joshua Barrie and Tristan Cork, 'How Taxpayers Were Still Paying for British Slave Trade Nearly 200 Years Later', *Mirror*, 9 June 2020.
2 David Olusoga, Twitter, 10 Feb. 2018, 9.10 a.m., x.com/DavidOlusoga/status/962252398273224705.
3 David Olusoga, 'The Treasury's Tweet Shows Slavery Is Still Misunderstood', *Guardian*, 12 Feb. 2018.
4 Tristan Cork, 'Taxpayers in Bristol Were Still Paying Debt to City's Slave Owners in 2015, Treasury Admits', *Bristol Post*, 13 Feb. 2018.
5 Information Rights Unit, 'Freedom of Information Act 2000: Slavery Abolition Act 1833', HM Treasury (letter), 31 Jan. 2018.
6 Lucy Mangan, 'Britain's Forgotten Slave Owners Review: "A Vivid Picture of the Spread of Slavery Profits"', *Guardian*, 23 July 2015.
7 Bertram Niles, 'UK Slavery Tweet Rekindles Caribbean Reparations Bid', CGTN, 27 Feb. 2018.
8 Tristan Cork, 'Petition Demands British Government Refunds Taxpayer the Money that Paid Off Slavery Debt', *Bristol Live*, 16 Feb. 2018.
9 Cleo Lake, 'Refund Our Taxes Paid to Compensate Enslavers!', Change.org, 16 Feb. 2018.

3: HUMPTY DUMPTY'S PROBLEM WITH DEFINITIONS
1 Ben Radley, 'Afrika and Reparations Activism in the UK: An Interview with Esther Stanford-Xosei', ROAPE.net, 10 March 2022.

4: THE END OF RACISM
1 'Sky Commits £30m to Support the Fight Against Racial Injustice and Invest More in Diversity and Inclusion', Sky (press release), 8 June 2020.
2 Panayiota Tsatsou, Nina Robinson, Joanna Abeyie and Aurora Herrera, *BBC Creative Diversity Commitment: A Report on the Impact of the BBC's £112 million Creative Diversity Commitment*, Sir Lenny Henry Centre for Media Diversity, March 2024.
3 Chanté Joseph, 'How to Help Close the Racial Wealth Gap', Chase UK (blog), 8 April 2024.
4 Office for National Statistics, 'Unemployment rate in the United Kingdom as of 3rd quarter 2024, by ethnic group', Statista Research Department, 13 Nov. 2024, statista.com/statistics/1123370/unemployment-rate-in-the-united-kingdom-uk/.
5 Randeep Ramesh, 'More Black People Jailed in England and Wales proportionally than in US', *Guardian*, 11 Oct. 2010.
6 Emma Dench, 'Roman Identity', in Alessandro Barchiesi and Walter Scheidel (eds), *The Oxford Handbook of Roman Studies*, OUP, 2010, p. 273.
7 Geraldine Heng, 'Race and Racism in the European Middle Ages', *Getty Iris*, 6 March 2019.

5: WHAT DID SLAVERY EVER DO FOR US?
1 Gillian Brockell, 'Before 1619, there Was 1526: The Mystery of the First Enslaved Africans in what Became the United States', *Washington Post*, 7 Sept. 2019.
2 Jasper Jolly, 'Barclays, HSBC and Lloyds among UK Banks that Had Links to Slavery', *Guardian*, 18 June 2020.

6: DOING THE MATHS
1 Coleman Bazelon, Alberto Vargas, Rohan Janakiraman and Mary M. Olson, *Report on Reparations for Transatlantic Chattel Slavery in the Americas and the Caribbean*, Brattle Group, 2023.

NOTES

7: REPARATIONS VERSUS CHARITY

1 'Our Full Statement on the Lloyd's Market's Role in the Slave Trade', Lloyds (press release), 18 June 2020.
2 'Pub Chain and Insurance Hub "Sorry" for Slave Links', BBC News, 18 June 2020.
3 Aamna Mohdin, '*Guardian* Owner Apologises for Founders' Links to Transatlantic Slavery', *Guardian*, 28 March 2023.
4 'The Scott Trust Legacies of Enslavement Report', *Guardian*, 28 March 2023.
5 The definition is from LexisNexis.
6 Aamna Mohdin, 'Laura Trevelyan Quits BBC to Campaign for Reparative Justice for Caribbean', *Guardian*, 16 March 2023.
7 CARICOM Reparations Commission (CRC), 'CARICOM Ten Point Plan for Reparatory Justice', caricom.org.

8: MAKING WAKANDA A REALITY

1 CARICOM, 'Barbados Prime Minister Calls for a Reparations "Caribbean Marshall Plan"', caricom.org, 14 July 2020.
2 'A Lecture by Mia Amor Mottley, Prime Minister of Barbados', LSE Events, 6 Dec. 2023.
3 Owen Bowcott and Ian Cobain, 'UK Sternly Resists Paying Reparations for Slave Trade Atrocities and Injustices', *Guardian*, 24 Feb. 2014.
4 Lennox Yieke, 'The Rise of Global Africa: Africa and the Caribbean Forge New Economic Partnership', *African Business*, 3 July 2024.
5 CARICOM Reparations Commission, '10-Point Reparation Plan', 2016, caricomreparations.org/caricom/caricoms-10-point-reparation-plan/.
6 'The 2023 Corruption Perceptions Index', Transparency International, [n.d.], transparency.org/en/cpi/2023.

10: THE TRILLION-DOLLAR QUESTION (PLUS ANOTHER 20-ISH TRILLION)

1 The Advocacy Team and Development Reimagined, *Making Finance for Reparations and Loss and Damage a Reality: What are the Options?*, Development Reimagined, 2023.

11: THE NAME'S LENNY, SPELT WITH A SILENT 'K'

1 Neha Gohil, 'Six in 10 in UK Poll say Descendants of Enslaved People Owed Formal Apology', *Guardian*, 25 March 2024.

12: WHAT NEXT?

1 Omar Khan, *The Colour of Money: How Racial Inequalities Obstruct a Fair and Resilient Economy*, Runnymede Trust, 2020.
2 Office for National Statistics, 'Unemployment rate in the United Kingdom as of 3rd quarter 2024, by ethnic group', Statista Research Department, 13 Nov. 2024.
3 Chris Parr, 'Number of Black Professors Up but Diversity Progress "Too Slow"', *Research Professional News*, 16 Jan. 2024.
4 Vikram Dodd, 'Black People Seven Times More Likely to Die after Police Restraint in Britain, Figures Show', *Guardian*, 19 Feb. 2023.
5 Aamna Mohdin, 'Black Women in UK Four Times More Likely to Die in Pregnancy and Childbirth', *Guardian*, 11 Nov. 2021.
6 'Black People Are More Than Three Times as Likely to Experience Homelessness', Shelter England (press release), 1 Oct. 2020.
7 Niamh McIntyre, Nazia Parveen and Tobi Thomas, 'Exclusion Rates Five Times Higher for Black Caribbean Pupils in Parts of England', *Guardian*, 24 March 2021.
8 Joe Stafford, 'Over a Third of People from Minority Groups Have Experienced Racist Assaults, Survey Finds', University of Manchester News, 19 April 2023.
9 'Facts and Figures about Racism and Mental Health', Mind, [n.d.], mind.org.uk/about-us/our-strategy/becoming-a-truly-anti-racist-organisation/facts-and-figures-about-racism-and-mental-health/.
10 'Facts and Figures about Racism and Mental Health', Mind.
11 The five permanent members are China, France, the Russian Federation, the United Kingdom and the United States.
12 Of the eight countries forming the G8, Italy, France, Germany, Canada, the UK and the USA all took part in the transatlantic slave trade, and Japan and Russia did not.
13 Suzanne Ackley, '5 Facts About Poverty in the Caribbean', Borgen Project, 19 Aug. 2023, borgenproject.org/poverty-in-the-caribbean/.
14 'Poverty Rates in Latin America Remain Above Pre-Pandemic Levels in 2022, ECLAC Warns', ECLAC (press release), 24 Nov. 2022, cepal.org/en/pressreleases/poverty-rates-latin-america-remain-above-pre-pandemic-levels-2022-eclac-warns.
15 Nonso Onwuta, '"Our Generation Will End Racism"', *Huck*, 11 June 2020.